·BUILD·IT·BETTER·YOURSELF·
WOODWORKING PROJECTS

Country Furniture
Living Rooms and Dens

D0564814

Collected and Written
by Nick Engler

Rodale Press
Emmaus, Pennsylvania

Printed in the United States of America

Series Editor: William H. Hylton
Managing Editor/Author: Nick Engler
Graphic Designer: Linda Watts
Graphic Artist: Christine Vogel
Draftspersons: Mary Jane Favorite
                Chris Walendzak
Photography: Karen Callahan
Cover Photography: Mitch Mandel
Typesetting: Computer Typography, Huber Heights, Ohio
Illustrations by O'Neil & Associates, Dayton, Ohio
Produced by Bookworks, Inc., West Milton, Ohio

If you have any questions or comments concerning this book, please write:
Rodale Press
Book Reader Service
33 East Minor Street
Emmaus, PA 18098

Library of Congress Cataloging-in-Publication Data

Engler, Nick.
    Country furniture : living rooms and dens /
collected and written by Nick Engler.
        p.   cm. – (Build-it-better-yourself
        woodworking projects)
    ISBN 0-87857-838-2 hardcover
    ISBN 0–87857 –853–6 paperback
    1. Woodwork.   2. Country furniture.   I. Title.
    II. Series.
TT180.E64   1989
684.1'04 – dc19   89-5956
                                             CIP

Distributed in the book trade by St. Martin's Press

2   4   6   8   10   9   7   5   3   hardcover
2   4   6   8   10   9   7   5   3   1   paperback

Contents

From the Keeping Room to the Living Room

As you set out to build country furniture for your living room or den, reflect on this irony: There were no living rooms or dens in eighteenth- and early nineteenth-century country homes. Both rooms are twentieth-century developments, products of changing lifestyles and an improving standard of living.

The contemporary living room descended from the Victorian parlor, where the members of a late nineteenth-century family might receive guests, play games and music, or spend the evenings. The den evolved from the Victorian study, where the adults might retire to read, write, or do the household accounting. Both the parlor and the study were results of the affluence generated by the Industrial Revolution. Only half a century earlier, such rooms were luxuries affordable to a very few.

Yet all but the poorest houses in colonial America had areas that served the same purposes as living rooms and parlors. A family newly arrived in America usually built a one-room cabin in which all huddled together. After several years, when they had established a farm and guaranteed themselves a future in the New World, the settlers enlarged their cramped quarters. They added a kitchen, a pantry, bedrooms, and other specialized rooms. The original cabin became a passageway to other areas of the expanding home. Even if they tore down their old cabin to build a larger house, the settlers designed it along the same lines — a central room or entranceway leading to other rooms.

The family used this central room for many different household and social activities — dining, sewing, reading, entertaining, or just passing the time. Family members moved their personal effects to their own bedrooms, but they kept things owned in common — dishes, linens, books, hunting rifles, and so on — centrally located. Because of everything stored in it, the central room became known as the keeping room.

Keeping room furniture was not dominated by any one type. There was usually a cupboard, a dresser, or a pewter bench to hold eating utensils. Chests of various sizes stored bedding and other cloth goods. If the head of the family was literate, or his profession demanded writing or bookkeeping, he might have a writing desk. There was always a lap desk or Bible box to store the family Bible. In the center of the room was usually a large dining table, ringed by chairs and settees. Around the perimeter were occasional tables for serving food and other activities. If there was an older person in the household, one or more of the chairs might be a rocker; the rocking chair, an invention of American country craftsmen, was thought to provide physical therapy for the elderly.

Though the architectural forms are separated by two centuries, much keeping room furniture works well in today's living rooms. Some of the designs are timeless: Settees, occasional tables, and writing desks still serve their original purposes. Other pieces have been adapted. Pewter benches now store books and collectibles. Lap desks organize bills, coupons, and other small items. Rocking chairs are enjoyed by the young as well as the old.

Some furniture has been imported from other areas of the house. Wardrobes and linen presses that once stored clothes in country bedrooms now hold televisions and stereo receivers. The low, sit-down workbenches that were the center of every country craftsmen's workshop have been converted to coffee tables. Even some outdoor pieces have been brought inside; whirligigs and weathervanes are displayed in living rooms as examples of folk art.

Whatever the mix of furniture, many of the doings in the twentieth-century living room or den remain the same as those in an eighteenth-century keeping room. Both are comfortable, sociable rooms where, as a day winds down, family members gather to relax and enjoy one another's company. The down-home look and feel of country living room furniture (though technically there isn't any such thing) nourishes this communal warmth.

Joiner's Wing-and-Arm Chair

Country chairs evolved from two different medieval woodworking traditions. Most familiar to us is the "turner's" chair, which was assembled of parts "thrown" on a lathe. Windsor chairs and Shaker rockers are examples of the turner's tradition.

"Joiner's" chairs are less familiar. The parts were ordinary boards and planks, cut with a saw. Five-board benches, settles, table-chairs, and similar kinds of country seating were built with planks and boards. The joiner's tradition survives today in upholstered arm-chairs and sofas. Springs, webbing, and batting have replaced the broad planks, but many of the furniture forms remain the same.

The chair shown here is typical of the joiner's wing-and-arm chair, the ancestor of our uphol-stered wing chair. While the wings are strictly decorative today, they once added to the warmth and comfort of the coun-try folks who used these chairs. When facing a fire, their broad surfaces reflected heat onto the person sitting in the chair and protected them from cold drafts.

Wing-and-arm chairs were built in many differ-ent sizes. Some were padded with rugs, cushions, or throw pillows. Smaller chairs were sometimes used as step-stools and stands. You can make this particular chair for either a child or an adult, simply by adjusting the scale of the patterns and the dimen-sions on the drawings.

Materials List

FINISHED DIMENSIONS

PARTS

Child's Chair

A.	Back	½″ x 9¼″ x 28″
B.	Sides (2)	½″ x 12″ x 26″
C.	Seat	½″ x 10¾″ x 12½″
D.	Apron	½″ x 3½″ x 12″
E.	Brace	½″ x 1½″ x 8⅞″

Adult's Chair

A.	Back	¾″ x 18¼″ x 56″
B.	Sides (2)	¾″ x 24″ x 52″
C.	Seat	¾″ x 21½″ x 24¾″
D.	Apron	¾″ x 7″ x 24″
E.	Brace	¾″ x 3″ x 17¹¹⁄₁₆″

EXPLODED VIEW

HARDWARE

Child's Chair

#8 x 1″ Flathead wood screws (15)
#8 x 1″ Roundhead wood screws and
   flat washers (3 sets)

Adult's Chair

#10 x 1¼″ Flathead wood screws
   (20–24)
#10 x 1¼″ Roundhead wood screws and
   flat washers (3 sets)

1

Determine the size of the chair. You can make this project to fit either a child or an adult. The drawings show a child-sized chair; an adult's chair would be twice as large.

If you make this chair for a child, use the dimensions on the drawings. If you build it for an adult, double the *overall* dimensions and use ¾″ stock (rather than ½″). In turn, cut the dadoes and grooves ¾″-wide and ⅜″-deep (rather than ½″ by ¼″), enlarge the patterns so that one square equals 1″ (rather than ½″), and cut the parts to the sizes shown on the "Adult's Chair" Materials List.

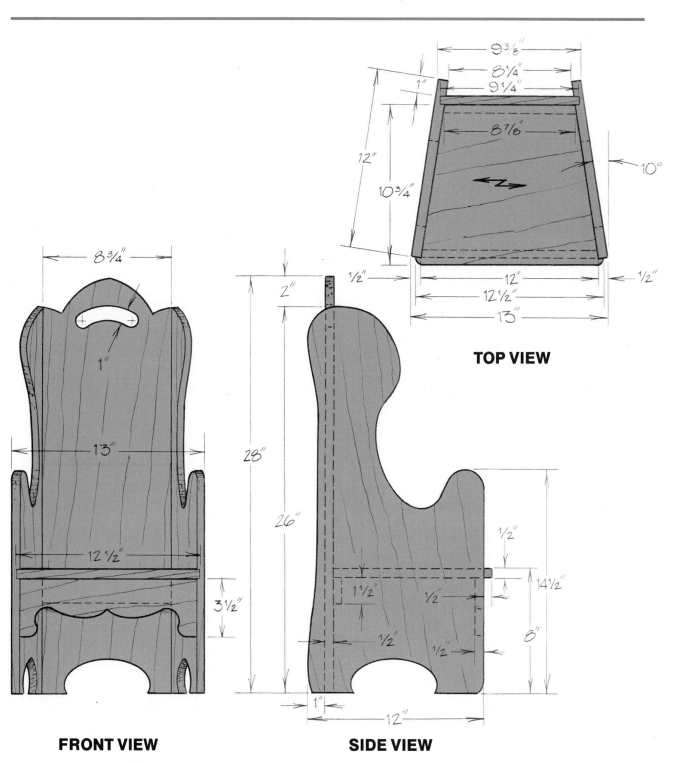

TOP VIEW

FRONT VIEW

SIDE VIEW

2 Cut the parts to size.

Cut the parts to size. To make this chair for a child, you'll need approximately 8 board feet of 4/4 (four quarters) stock, planed to ½″ thick. To make it for an adult, you'll need *four times* as much wood — 32 board feet — planed to ¾″ thick. Because the adult's chair requires so many wide boards, you may want to make it from cabinet-grade plywood. You can cover the edges with veneer tape to hide the plies.

If you're working with solid stock, glue up the wide boards you need. Join the edges with dowels, splines, or tongues and grooves to reinforce the glue joints. Then cut the sides and back to the sizes shown in the Materials List. Rip the seat, apron, and brace to the width you need, but crosscut them approximately 1″ longer than specified. This will allow you to fit them to the chair as it's assembled.

3 Cut the joinery in the chair sides.

Cut the joinery in the chair sides. You'll want to cut the dadoes and grooves *before* you cut the shape of the sides, so that you can orient them accurately. Cut the dado for the seat plank with either a dado cutter or a router. The groove for the back, however, *must* be made with a dado cutter, because this groove is cut at a bevel-like angle of 10°, as shown in the *Top View.* (See Figure 1.) As you cut these joints, remember that the chair sides should be *mirror images* of each other.

1/Cut the groove for the chair back using a dado cutter. After adjusting the cutter to the proper width and depth of cut, tilt the arbor (or table) to 10°. Then make the cut.

4 Cut the shapes of the sides, back, and apron.

Cut the shapes of the sides, back, and apron. Enlarge the *Side Pattern, Back Pattern,* and *Apron Pattern.* Trace these patterns onto the stock, and cut the shapes with a band saw or saber saw.

Make the handle cut-out in the back only if you are building the child's chair. Drill two 1″-diameter holes to mark the ends of the cut-out, then remove the waste in between the holes with a saber saw. Sand the sawed edges.

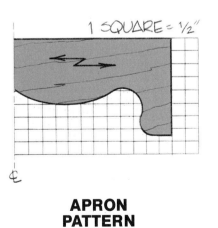

APRON PATTERN

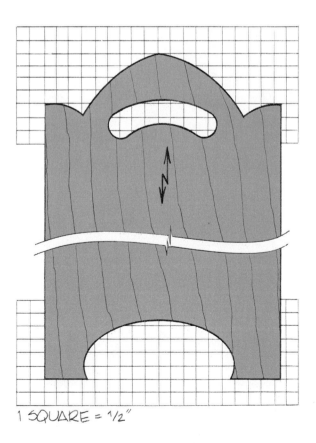

1 SQUARE = ½″

BACK PATTERN

TRY THIS! To make the chair as sturdy as possible, cut the seat to fit, rather than to the specifications on the Materials List. To start, cut the seat ⅛″–¼″ wider than specified. Then dry assemble the chair. Carefully determine how much stock you have to trim from the seat. Readjust the rip fence on your table saw, and repeat the second taper cut, shaving the edge of the seat. When you reassemble the chair, all the parts should fit perfectly.

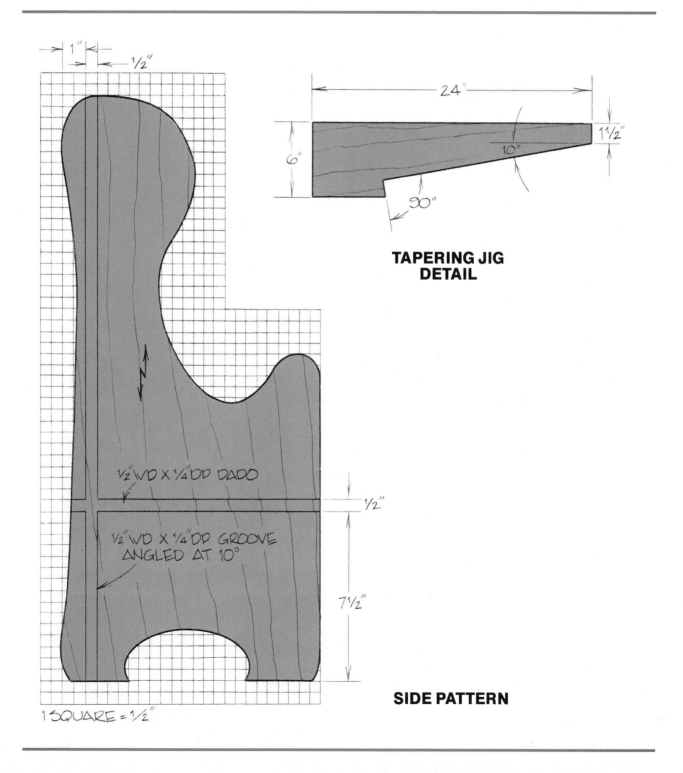

TAPERING JIG DETAIL

½″ WD X ¼″ DP DADO

½″ WD X ¼″ DP GROOVE ANGLED AT 10°

SIDE PATTERN

1 SQUARE = ½″

5

Taper the seat. The chair seat is trapezoid-shaped — it tapers 10°, front to back. Cut the tapered sides on a table saw, using a tapering jig. You can make this jig yourself by cutting a piece of scrap wood with a band saw or saber saw, as shown in the *Tapering Jig Detail*.

Carefully position the rip fence for the first cut and place the jig against it. Put the seat stock in the jig and push it forward into the blade, tapering one edge. Save the scrap.

Turn the stock over, side for side. Place the *scrap* in the jig, then butt the tapered edge of the seat stock against it. Readjust the position of the rip fence, and cut the second edge. (See Figure 2.)

2/When making the second taper cut, use the scrap from the first cut as a spacer to hold the stock at the proper angle to the blade.

6

Assemble the sides, back, and seat. Finish sand the sides, back, and seat. Glue the back and the seat to the sides, but don't glue the seat to the back. Reinforce the joints with flathead wood screws.

Counterbore and countersink the screws, then cover the heads with wooden plugs. (The seat isn't glued to the back because the grain directions of these two parts oppose each other, and the joint will break.)

7

Install the apron and the brace. Cut the apron and the brace to fit the chair assembly. Miter the ends at 10°, cutting them so the pieces are just a little long. Then trim one end of each $\frac{1}{32}$″-$\frac{1}{16}$″ at a time. Each time you cut it, check the fit. When the piece fits just right, attach it to the chair.

The brace is attached to the back with roundhead wood screws and flat washers, and to the underside of the seat with glue. Do *not* glue the brace to the back because their grains oppose each other. Instead, drill oversized shank holes in the brace. This will keep the brace securely in place, yet allow the back to expand and contract.

Finish sand the apron, then glue it to the sides and the underside of the seat. Reinforce the glue with flathead wood screws. Counterbore and countersink these screws, then hide the heads with wooden plugs.

8

Finish the chair. Do any touch-up sanding necessary. With a file and sandpaper, blend the top edge of the back into the curved shapes of the sides. (See Figure 3.) If you built the chair from plywood, apply veneer tape to all the visible edges. If you made it from solid wood, break all the edges with a scraper and sandpaper to give the chair a worn appearance.

Apply a finish to the completed chair. Typically, joiners' chairs were painted bright colors. Whatever finish you use, be sure to coat *all* surfaces equally to keep the boards from warping.

You can cut pieces of foam rubber to fit the seat and the back, then cover the foam with fabric, making cushions. If you sew cord to the cushions and drill holes in the chair at suitable locations, you can tie them in place.

3/Blend the top edges of the sides and the back together, so that the contours of the chair appear continuous. Round the edges, too. This blending and rounding is important to soften what would otherwise be a very angular design.

Occasional Table

Occasional tables were, perhaps, the most versatile pieces of furniture in a country home. Put into service whenever and wherever an occasion demanded extra table space, these small tables could be used as sideboards, game tables, workbenches, writing desks, lamp stands — the list is endless. Today, they often serve as side tables, beside a chair or a couch.

Occasional tables were constructed simply, usually just four legs and a top joined by a frame. The legs might have been turned, tapered, or straight, depending on the preferences of the craftsman who made them. The tables were often made with one or two small drawers, used to store eating utensils, game boards, hand tools, or writing materials.

The 150-year-old table shown here is typical of many country occasional tables. Four turned legs are mortised to hold the tenons of the aprons. The drawer slides on L-shaped guides attached to the aprons, and the top is held to the leg-and-apron assembly with wooden clips. There's nothing particularly fancy about the design or the joinery, but after almost a century and a half, the table is still solid, attractive, and useful.

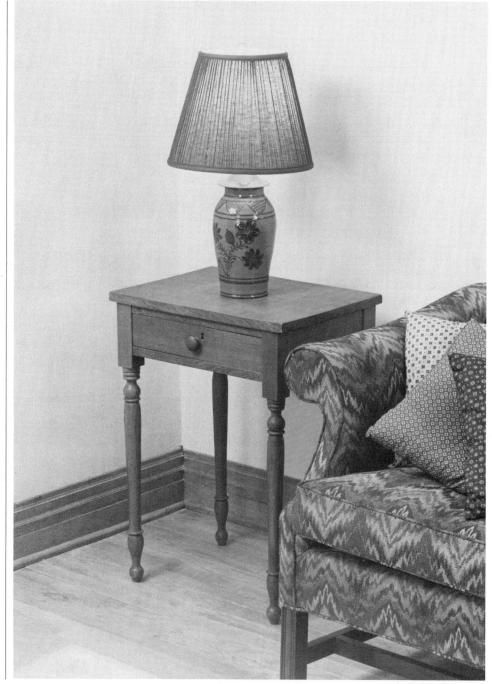

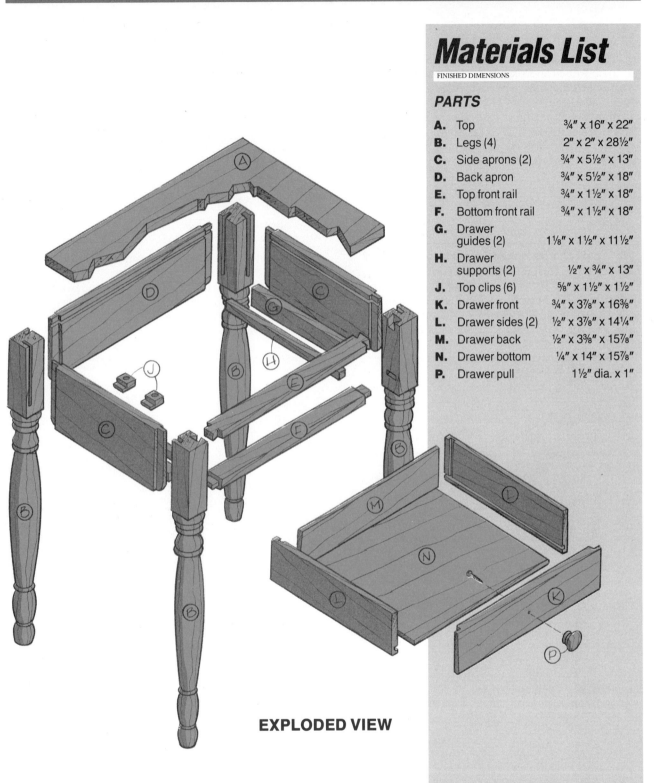

EXPLODED VIEW

Materials List

FINISHED DIMENSIONS

PARTS

A.	Top	¾" x 16" x 22"
B.	Legs (4)	2" x 2" x 28½"
C.	Side aprons (2)	¾" x 5½" x 13"
D.	Back apron	¾" x 5½" x 18"
E.	Top front rail	¾" x 1½" x 18"
F.	Bottom front rail	¾" x 1½" x 18"
G.	Drawer guides (2)	1⅛" x 1½" x 11½"
H.	Drawer supports (2)	½" x ¾" x 13"
J.	Top clips (6)	⅝" x 1½" x 1½"
K.	Drawer front	¾" x 3⅞" x 16⅜"
L.	Drawer sides (2)	½" x 3⅞" x 14¼"
M.	Drawer back	½" x 3⅜" x 15⅞"
N.	Drawer bottom	¼" x 14" x 15⅞"
P.	Drawer pull	1½" dia. x 1"

HARDWARE

#10 x 1¼" Flathead wood screws (9)

1

Cut the parts to size. To build this project, you'll need approximately 8 board feet of 4/4 (four-quarters) stock, 4 board feet of 10/4 (ten-quarters) stock, and a small piece (14" x 16", approximately) of ¼" plywood. Plane the 4/4 stock to 3/4" thick and the 10/4 stock to 2" thick. Then cut all the parts of the table, with the exception of the drawer pull, to the sizes shown in the Materials List.

> **TRY THIS!** Ask if your lumberyard has 2" x 2" table-leg turning squares already made up. Many do, and if this is the case, you won't have to purchase 10/4 material and plane it down. Remember to buy an extra turning square to make the drawer guides.

2

Cut the dovetails on the upper front rail. The upper front rail is joined to the legs by dovetail tenons. These tenons should be cut *before* you make the dovetail mortises so you can use them as a template to lay out the mortises. (All the other tenons should be made *after* the mortises so you can fit them

to the mortises.) Mark the shape and cut it out with a band saw, then file the edges smooth.

The upper front rail is fastened to the top by two #10 x 1¼" flathead wood screws. Before you set this part aside, drill and countersink the pilot holes shown on the *Frame/Top View.*

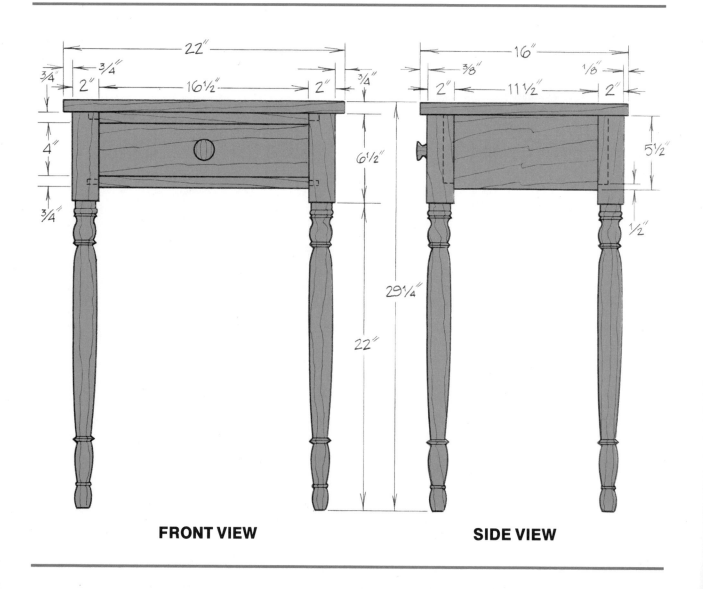

FRONT VIEW   **SIDE VIEW**

3

Cut the mortises into the legs. The legs and aprons are joined by slot mortises and tenons. Cut these mortises with a table-mounted router, using a ¼″ straight bit. The mortises must be cut ¼″ wide, ¾″ deep, and 5″ long. (See Figure 1.) Each mortise must be cut on the *inside* face of the stock, ⅜″ in from the adjacent *outside* face, as shown in the *Apron-to-Leg Joinery Detail.* Cut one slot mortise in each front leg and two in each back leg.

To cut the mortises safely, be sure you feed the stock from right to left (as you stand facing the tool, with the bit between you and the fence). This way, the rotation of the bit will help force the stock against the fence. Rout each mortise in several passes, cutting just ⅛″-¼″ deeper with each pass. To control the length of the cut, clamp a stop block to the fence at the appropriate location to the left of the bit. Set the fence ⅜″ from the bit, and cut one mortise in each leg. Then set the fence 1⅜″ from the bit, and cut the second mortise in each of the back legs.

The front legs must also be mortised for the front rails. The upper mortise is a dovetail-shaped recess, while the lower mortise is rectangular. Carefully mark the joints on the stock, using the dovetail tenons that you have already made to mark the upper mortises. Remove as much of the waste as you can from each mortise with a drill. Clean up the corners and the edges of the mortises with a chisel. (See Figure 2.)

Alternative method: If you don't have a router table, you can also make the mortises with a dado cutter. Use a fence to guide the stock and a stop block to stop the cut, just as you would with a router.

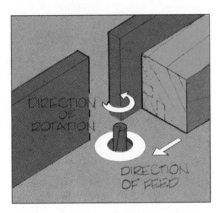

1/Most woodworkers have learned that power tool shafts rotate clockwise. But mount the router in a router table — it is upside down now — and its shaft rotates counterclockwise. Consequently, for the most safety, feed the stock into the cutter from right to left. The bit rotation helps force the stock against the fence.

*2/To make the mortises in the legs for the front rails, drill a series of **stopped** holes to remove the waste, then clean up the sides of the mortise with a chisel. A **Forstner** bit is best for this operation, since it cuts a hole with a perfectly flat bottom.*

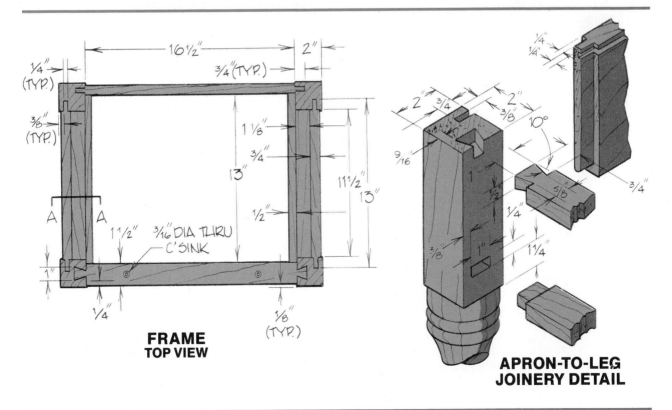

**FRAME
TOP VIEW**

**APRON-TO-LEG
JOINERY DETAIL**

4

Cut the tenons on the aprons and the lower front rail. You can cut the tenons in the aprons and the lower front rail with a table-mounted router. Mount a ¾″ straight bit in the tool. Adjust the fence position and the bit height to cut a ¾″-wide,

¼″-deep rabbet as you pass the stock across the bit. To make the apron tenons, cut one face, turn the board over, and cut the other. (See Figure 3.) For the front rail, cut all four sides — faces and edges. Using a rasp, round the lower edge of the apron tenons to fit the mortise, as shown in the *Apron Tenon Detail/End View.*

Alternative method: Once again, you can use a dado cutter to make the tenons if you don't have a router table. You can also use an ordinary saw blade and a tenoning jig.

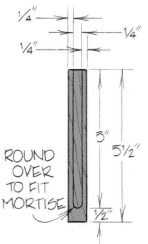

APRON TENON DETAIL
END VIEW

3/When cutting the tenons on a router table, use a miter gauge to help keep the stock square to the fence.

5

Turn the legs. After you have cut and fitted all the mortises and tenons, turn the legs. (Don't turn the legs until you have cut *all* the joinery. You'll find it almost impossible to cut square joints after the legs have been shaped.) A suggested design is shown in the

Leg Pattern. Design your own turning, if you wish. You don't even have to turn the leg. Country cabinetmakers made square tapered legs (in imitation of Federal furniture styles) or square straight legs (in imitation of the Chippendale style).

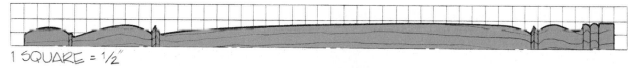

1 SQUARE = ½″

LEG PATTERN

6

Turn the drawer pull. While you're set up to work at the lathe, make the pull. This is a *faceplate* turning. Glue the stock to a ¾″-thick scrap of wood with a sheet of paper in between the stock and the scrap. Mount the stock on the faceplate by driving screws into the scrap. After turning the pull as shown in the *Drawer Pull Pattern,* separate the pull from the scrap by placing a chisel at the seam between the two pieces of wood and striking it sharply with a mallet. Because of the paper in the glue joint, the pull and the scrap will part cleanly and easily.

Note: The pull's wood grain should parallel the turning axis. It's very difficult to turn stock when the grain runs side to side.

DRAWER PULL
PATTERN

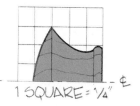

1 SQUARE = ¼″

7

Cut grooves in the aprons and make the clips. The table top is held to the aprons by six wooden clips. With its tongue fitted into a groove in the apron, each clip is screwed to the underside of the top as shown in *Section A*. This arrangement allows the top to expand and contract with changes in the weather.

To make the clips, sand or plane a wide board to ⅝″ thick. Across one end, cut a ⅜″-wide, ⁵⁄₁₆″-deep rabbet. Cut a 1½″-long piece off the board, then rip that piece into 1½″ squares. (See Figure 4.) Repeat as necessary until you have six clips.

With a router and a ⅜″ straight bit, plow a ⅜″-wide, ⅜″-deep groove, ⅜″ from the upper edge of the aprons. (You could also use a dado cutter to make this groove.) The clips' tongues should fit loosely in these grooves.

*4/Make the clips by cutting a rabbet across the end of a board, then cutting the board up into squares. The grain direction of each clip **must** be perpendicular to the rabbet. Otherwise, the clips may break.*

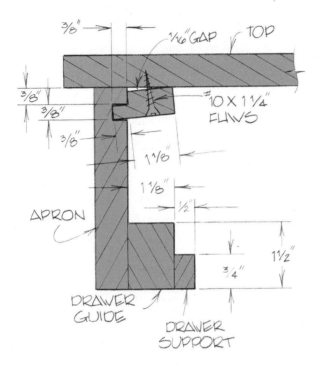

SECTION A

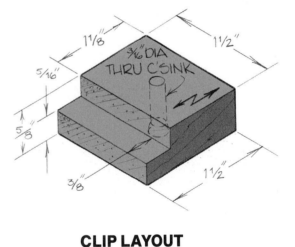

CLIP LAYOUT

8

Finish sand the parts of the table. Finish sand all of the parts that will show — top, legs, aprons, and rails. (If you have turned the legs, sand the round surfaces on the lathe.) You don't need to smooth the clips, drawer guides, or drawer supports since they won't be visible in the completed project.

9

Attach the drawer guides and supports to the side aprons. Glue the drawer guides and supports together to make two L-shaped brackets. When the glue sets, attach these brackets to the inside face of the side aprons. The bottom edge of the brackets should be flush with the bottom edge of the aprons, and the ends of the brackets should be flush with the shoulders of the tenons.

10

Assemble the table. Dry assemble the table to check the fit of the joints. If a joint is too tight, pare stock away from the mortises or the tenons. If it's too loose, use paper or scraps of veneer to shim it. When you're satisfied with the fit, reassemble the legs, aprons, and rails with glue.

After the glue dries, attach the top to the aprons with clips and flathead wood screws. Complete the installation by driving two screws through the upper front rail and into the top. The shank holes in the rail should be slightly larger than the shanks of the screws. This will allow the top to expand and contract properly.

11

Build the drawer. The sides are joined to the drawer front by rabbets, and to the back by dadoes. The drawer bottom floats in a groove in the front and sides. Cut the rabbets, dadoes, and grooves with a router or dado cutter.

Dry assemble the drawer to check the fit of the parts. If the fit is satisfactory, reassemble the front, back, and sides with glue. Reinforce the glue joints with 4d finishing nails, and set the nail heads below the surface of the wood. Slide the bottom in place and nail it to the bottom edge of the back. Do *not* glue it in its grooves or nail it to any part. Let it float free in the grooves. Be sure the drawer is square as you assemble it; otherwise it may not fit or slide properly.

Lightly sand the drawer. Attach the pull to the drawer by driving a screw through the front and into the back of the pull. Test fit the drawer in the table. If it rubs or binds, plane a little stock off the areas that seem to be sticking. When the drawer slides easily, rub the bottom edges of the sides with paraffin. This will help the drawer work smoothly.

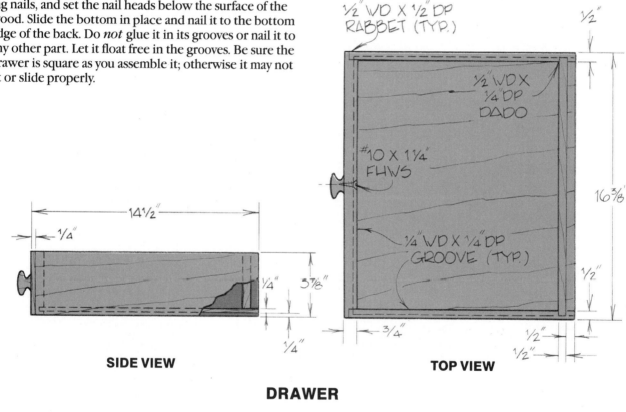

SIDE VIEW

TOP VIEW

DRAWER

12

Finish the completed table. Remove the drawer from the table. Do any necessary touch-up sanding to the surfaces that still need it, then apply a finish to the project. Be certain to apply as many coats of finish to the underside of the table top as you

do to the topside — this will help keep it from warping. Do *not,* however, finish the drawer assembly other than the face. Traditionally, the insides of drawers are left raw so that they will absorb moisture and odors from their contents.

Writing Desk

The desk, as we know it, is a fairly recent development. Until the beginning of the nineteenth century, the typical country family could keep all of its important papers, letters, writing materials — its entire *library* — in a small box. The first desks were, in fact, boxes like the Lap Desk shown later in this book.

But education was nurtured and encouraged in the American colonies. As the public became more literate, families outgrew their desk boxes. At first they simply made them larger and put legs on them. Then they began to add drawers, cabinet space, and pigeonholes to help organize their paperwork. Various types of desks began to appear — secretary, drop-lid, bureau, and so on.

A popular early desk design was a cabinet on a table. Country folk favored this design because it was practical and easy to make. The table was an ordinary worktable, and the cabinet was a chest with small drawers and dividers. Oftentimes, the table top was made to fold up when the desk wasn't being used. A homespun name was coined to match the design. It was called a writing desk. ●

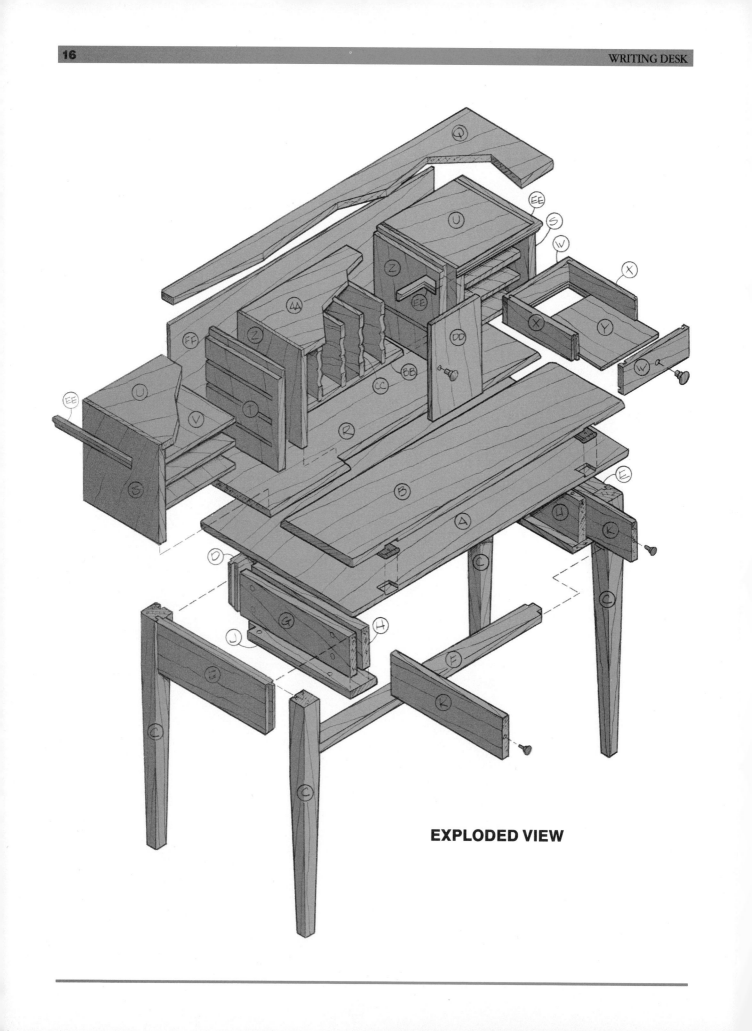

EXPLODED VIEW

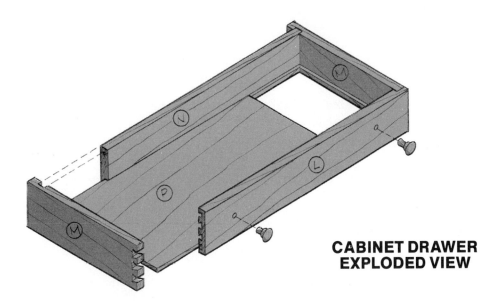

**CABINET DRAWER
EXPLODED VIEW**

Materials List

FINISHED DIMENSIONS

PARTS

Table

A.	Table top	¾" x 18¼" x 33½"
B.	Drop leaf	¾" x 8⅜" x 33½"
C.	Legs (4)	1¾" x 1¾" x 27¾"
D.	Back apron	¾" x 5⅝" x 29"
E.	Side aprons (2)	¾" x 5⅝" x 14¾"
F.	Front stretcher	¾" x 1¾" x 29"
G.	Spacers (2)	¾" x 4⅞" x 13¾"
H.	Dividers (2)	¾" x 4⅞" x 16⅝"
J.	Ledgers (2)	¾" x 3" x 14½"
K.	Drop leaf supports (2)	⅝" x 4¹³⁄₁₆" x 16¼"
L.	Large drawer front	¾" x 4¾" x 24⅞"
M.	Large drawer sides (2)	¾" x 4¾" x 15⅞"
N.	Large drawer back	¾" x 4¾" x 24⅛"
P.	Large drawer bottom	¼" x 15" x 24⅛"

Cabinet

Q.	Cabinet top	¾" x 10¼" x 34"
R.	Cabinet bottom	¾" x 9¾" x 33"
S.	Drawer section outside sides (2)	¾" x 9" x 10"
T.	Drawer section inside sides (2)	¾" x 8¾" x 10"
U.	Drawer section tops (2)	¾" x 8" x 8¾"
V.	Small drawer supports (6)	½" x 8" x 8¼"
W.	Small drawer fronts/backs (16)	½" x 1⅞" x 7⅜"
X.	Small drawer sides (16)	¼" x 1⅞" x 7¾"
Y.	Small drawer bottoms (8)	⅛" x 7⅛" x 7¾"
Z.	Pigeonhole section sides (2)	¾" x 7¾" x 10"
AA.	Pigeonhole section top	¾" x 7¾" x 12½"
BB.	Pigeonhole shelf	½" x 7" x 12½"
CC.	Pigeonhole dividers (4)	¼" x 6" x 7"
DD.	Pigeonhole doors (2)	½" x 5⅞" x 9⅞"
EE.	Cabinet molding (total)	½" x ½" x 60"
FF.	Cabinet back	¼" x 10" x 30½"

HARDWARE

Small door/drawer pulls (12)
Large drawer pulls (2)
Table hinges and mounting screws (1 pair)
Bullet catches and striker plates (1 pair)
#10 x 1¼" Flathead wood screws (24–30)
#10 x 1¼" Roundhead wood screws (6)
#10 Washers
4d Finishing nails (12)
1" Brads (70–80)
1" Wire nails (2)

Building the Table

1 Cut the parts of the table to size. This is not a complex project, but there are lots of parts, as you can see by the Materials List. To avoid being overwhelmed, build the desk in two stages — first the table, then the cabinet. This will help you stay organized and will keep your shop from becoming too cluttered to work.

To build the table portion of the desk, you'll need approximately 15 board feet of 4/4 (four-quarters) stock, 4 board feet of 8/4 (eight-quarters) stock, and a quarter sheet (2' x 4') of ¼" plywood. Plane the 4/4 stock to ¾" thick, and the 8/4 stock to 1¾" thick. Then cut all the parts of the table to the sizes shown in the Materials List.

2 Cut the mortises in the legs. The legs and aprons are joined by slot mortises and tenons. You can make these mortises with a router or a dado cutter. Set up your machine to cut a ¼"-wide, ½"-deep groove, ½" from the *outside* face of each leg, as shown in the *Leg-to-Apron Joinery Detail*. To cut all six mortises, you will have to use two different fence settings. (See Figure 1.) Cut one slot mortise in each leg, then reset the fence and cut the second mortise in the back legs.

The front legs must also be mortised for the front stretcher. Carefully lay out the mortises on the stock, then rough them out, removing as much waste as you can with a drill. Square up the mortises with a chisel. (See Figure 2.)

1/Clamp a block to the fence to stop the cut when it is exactly 5⅝" long.

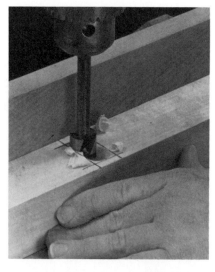

2/To rough out the mortises in the legs for the front stretcher, drill a series of **stopped** holes to remove the waste. A **Forstner** bit is best for this operation, since it leaves a hole with a perfectly flat bottom. Complete the mortise by squaring the sides and the corners with a chisel.

3 Cut the tenons on the aprons and the front stretcher. You can do this with a router or a dado cutter. Set up the machine to cut a ½"-wide, ¼"-deep rabbet in the edge of a board. To make each apron tenon, cut a rabbet across the end, turn the board over, and cut a second. (See Figure 3.) To make the tenons in the front stretcher, cut the rabbets in the edges. If you cut the mortises with a dado cutter, use a rasp to round the bottom corner of each apron tenon, as indicated in the *Leg-to-Apron Joinery Detail*.

3/When cutting the tenons on the aprons and the stretcher, use the miter gauge to keep the stock perpendicular to the fence.

4 ***Cut dadoes in the back apron.*** The inside face of the back apron is dadoed to accept the dividers, as shown in *Section B.* Using a router or a dado cutter, make two ¾″-wide, ⅜″-deep dadoes in the back apron, 1¼″ in from the ends of the tenons, as shown in the *Leg-to-Apron Joinery Detail.*

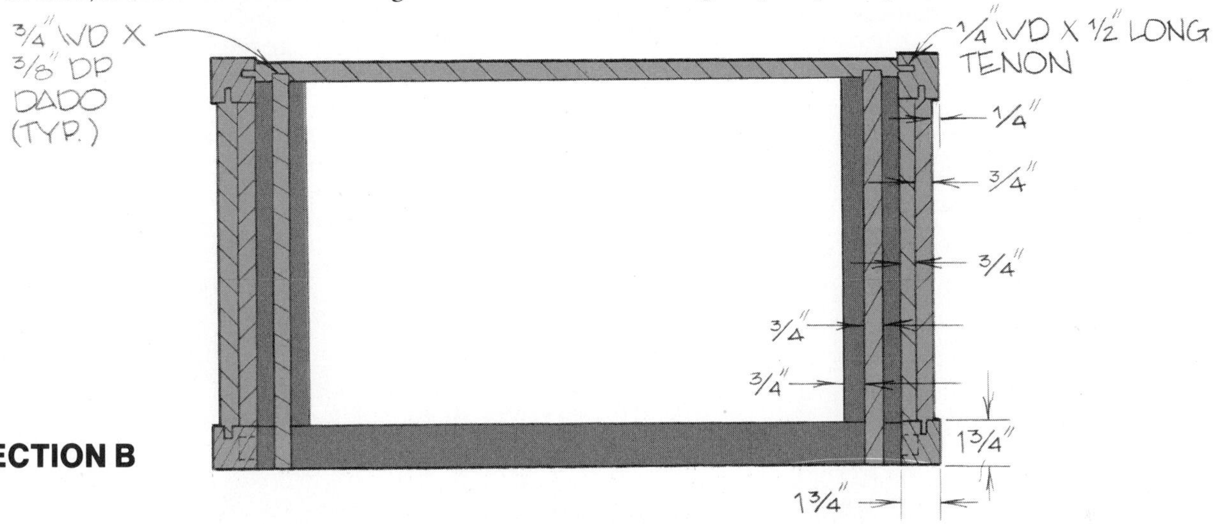

3/4" WD X 3/8" DP DADO (TYP.)
1/4" WD X 1/2" LONG TENON
1/4"
3/4"
3/4"
3/4"
3/4"
1 3/4"
1 3/4"

SECTION B

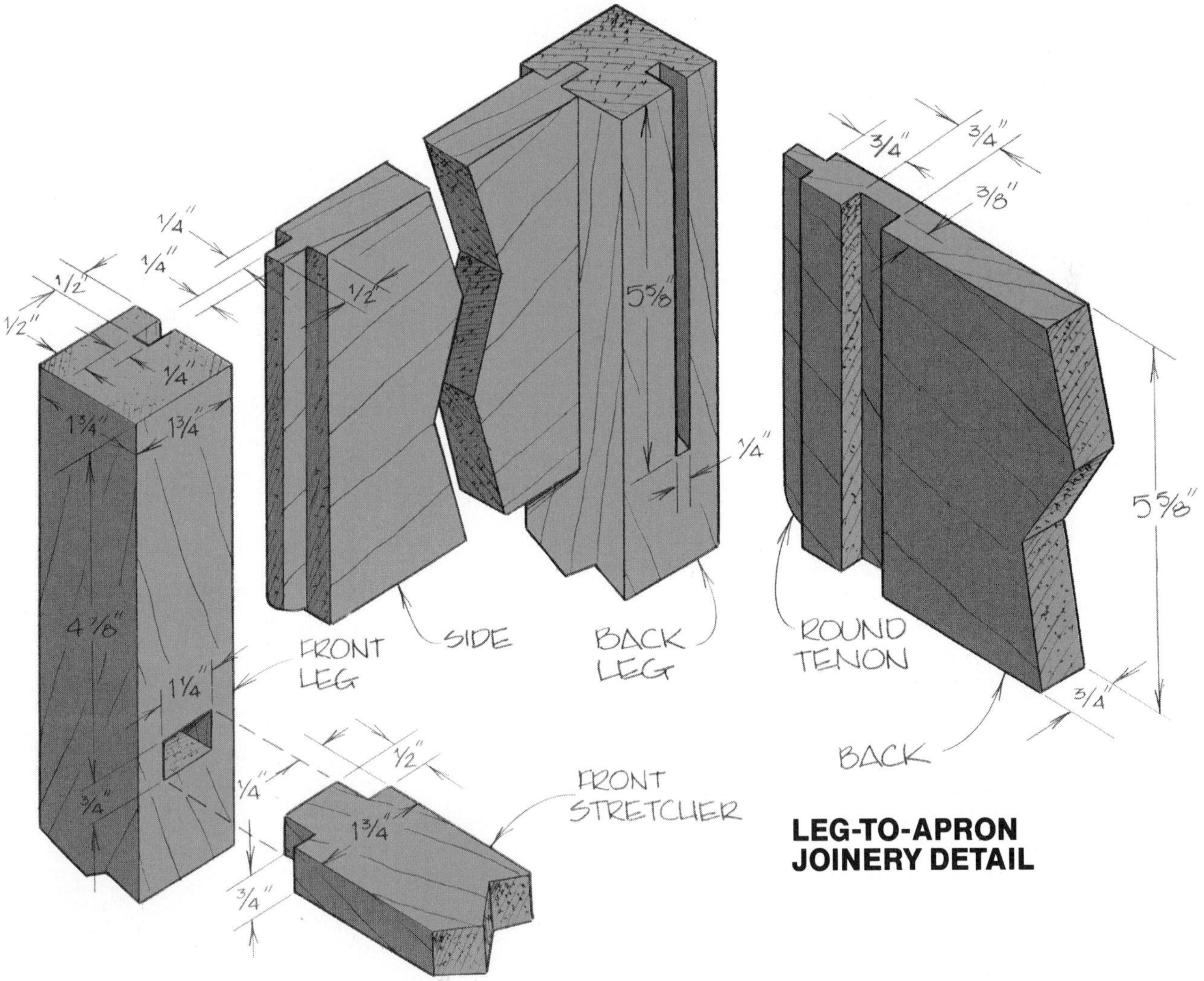

1/4"
1/4"
1/2"
1/2"
1/4"
1 3/4"
1 3/4"
1/2"
5 5/8"
1/4"
3/4"
3/4"
3/8"
5 5/8"
3/4"
4 7/8"
1 1/4"
3/4"
1/2"
1/4"
1 3/4"
3/4"
FRONT LEG
SIDE
BACK LEG
ROUND TENON
BACK
FRONT STRETCHER

LEG-TO-APRON JOINERY DETAIL

5

Drill screw pockets in the back apron and the dividers. The table top is secured to the table assembly with screws driven through screw pockets in the inside faces of the back apron and the

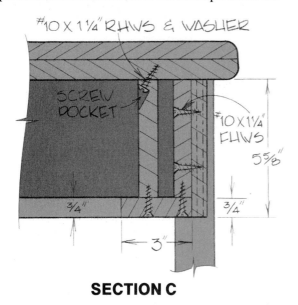

SECTION C

dividers, as shown in *Section C.* Make these pockets on your drill press. Tilt the worktable to 15°, and clamp a fence to it, ⅜″ from where the point of the bit touches the table. Protect the worktable with a scrap, then clamp the stock to the fence. Create the pocket with a ⅝″-diameter bit, drilling into the side of the stock and stopping ⅜″ above the table. Switch to a ³⁄₁₆″-diameter bit and drill through the stock. (See Figure 4.) The bit should exit from the center of the edge.

4/When you drill the pilot holes for the screws that secure the top in place, make the shank holes slightly larger than the shank of the screw. This will allow the top to expand and contract.

6

Taper the legs. After you have cut and fitted all the mortises and tenons, taper the legs as shown in the *Front View* and the *Side View.* The legs taper from 1¾″ square to 1″ square; the taper, which is cut only in the two inside faces of the legs, begins 6″ from the top. Cut these tapers on your table saw, using a tapering jig.

Note: Don't taper the legs until you have cut the mortises in them. You'll find it almost impossible to cut them accurately after the legs have been tapered.

TRY THIS! You can make your own tapering jig from a scrap of plywood, as shown in the illustration. This jig is designed to taper a board ¾″ over a rip cut 21¾″ long — the same taper needed for the writing desk legs.

Cut out the tapering jig with a band saw or saber saw. These tapers won't be quite straight, but the cuts you make with the aid of the jig will be.

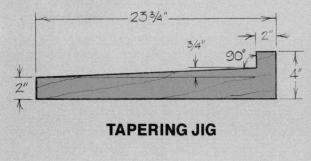

TAPERING JIG

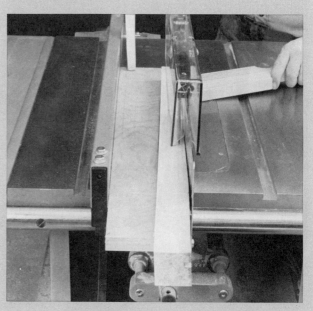

7

Make the drop-leaf supports. Plane the drop-leaf support stock to ⅝″ thick, so it will slide smoothly in and out of the table. Cut a ⅛″ relief along the top edges, as shown in the *Drop-Leaf Support Layout*. The easiest way to make this relief is on a jointer. Adjust the depth of cut to ⅛″, and pass the board over the knives as if you were jointing the edge. Stop the pass 2″ before you reach the end of the stock.

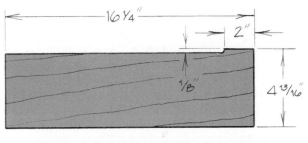

DROP-LEAF SUPPORT LAYOUT

8

Shape the edges of the top and drop leaf. With a router or a shaper, round over the bottom edges of the top and the drop leaf, as shown in the *Top Edge Profile*. Shape only the side edges of the top, leaving the front and back square. Shape the front and side edges of the drop leaf. Do not shape the back edge; leave it square.

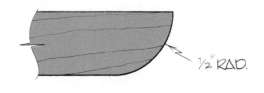

TABLE TOP EDGE PROFILE

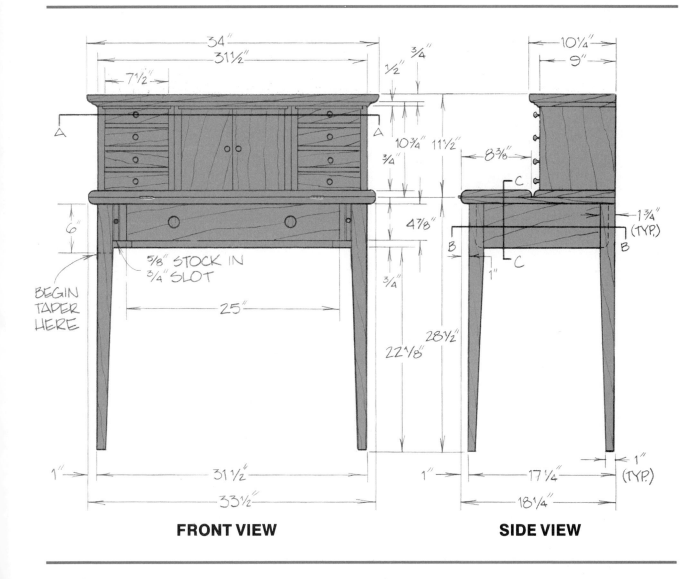

FRONT VIEW   **SIDE VIEW**

9

Assemble the table. Finish sand the parts of the table that will show — top, drop leaf, legs, aprons, stretcher, and dividers. Dry assemble the table. When you're satisfied that the joints fit properly, reassemble the legs, aprons, and stretcher with glue. Ensure that the assembly is square as you clamp it.

After the glue sets up on the leg/apron/stretcher assembly, attach the spacers to the side aprons with flathead wood screws. Glue the dividers to the back apron and the front stretcher, and screw the ledgers to the bottom edges of the spacers and the dividers. Attach the top to the assembly with roundhead wood screws and washers, driving the screws through the screw pockets in the dividers and the back apron.

Hinge the drop leaf to the top. Mortise the hinges so they are flush with the top surface of the table. Finally, install pulls on the ends of the supports and slide them into place between the dividers and the spacers.

10

Build and fit the desk drawer. The drawer sides and front are joined by half-blind dovetails, and the back fits in dadoes. The drawer bottom floats in a groove plowed in the sides, front, and back. Cut the dovetails with a router and a template, and the dadoes and grooves with a router or a dado cutter.

Finish sand the drawer parts, then dry assemble the drawer. If the joints fit satisfactorily, reassemble the front, back, and sides with glue. Do *not* glue the bottom in place; let it float in the grooves. Be sure the drawer is square as you assemble it; otherwise it may not fit the desk or slide properly.

Lightly sand the dovetails to clean them and make them flush. Attach the pulls, and test fit the drawer in the desk. If it binds, plane a little stock off the appropriate spot. When the drawer slides easily, rub the bottom edges of the sides with paraffin.

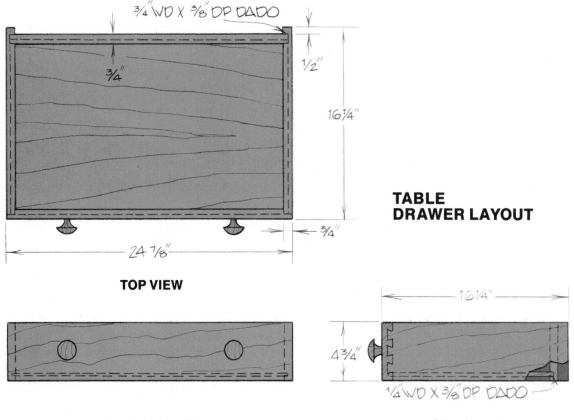

TABLE DRAWER LAYOUT

TOP VIEW

FRONT VIEW

SIDE VIEW

Building the Cabinet

11 ***Cut the parts of the cabinet to size.***
To make the cabinet, you'll need approximately 22 board feet of 4/4 stock and a quarter sheet (2′ x 4′) of ¼″ plywood. Plane 11 board feet of the solid stock to ¾″ thick, 7 board feet to ½″ thick, 2 board feet to ¼″ thick, and the remaining 2 board feet to ⅛″ thick. Then cut all the parts, with the exception of the moldings, to the sizes shown in the Materials List. You'll cut the moldings to size later.

Note: To get the *square* feet of ¼″- and ⅛″-thick material that you need from the *board* feet that we specified, you'll have to resaw the 4/4 stock on a band saw before you plane it. Resaw the stock into two pieces for the ¼″ wood, and into three pieces for the ⅛″ wood.

12 ***Cut the joinery in the cabinet parts.***
The cabinet consists of three units — two drawer units and a pigeonhole unit — joined by a back, top, and bottom. Each of these units is held together by dado and rabbet joints. Cut these dadoes and rabbets with either a router or a dado cutter, starting with the widest cut. Refer to the *Cabinet Drawer Unit/Outer Side Layout, Pigeonhole Side Layout,* and *Pigeonhole Top/Shelf Layout* for the position and dimensions of each joint:

- ¾″-wide, ¼″-deep rabbets in the drawer and pigeonhole sides to hold the tops
- ½″-wide, ¼″-deep blind dadoes in the drawer unit sides to hold the drawer supports
- ½″-wide, ¼″-deep blind dadoes in the pigeonhole sides to hold the shelf
- ¼″-wide, ¼″-deep dadoes in the pigeonhole shelf and top to hold the dividers
- ¼″-wide, ¼″-deep rabbets in the back edge of the outside drawer unit sides to hold the back

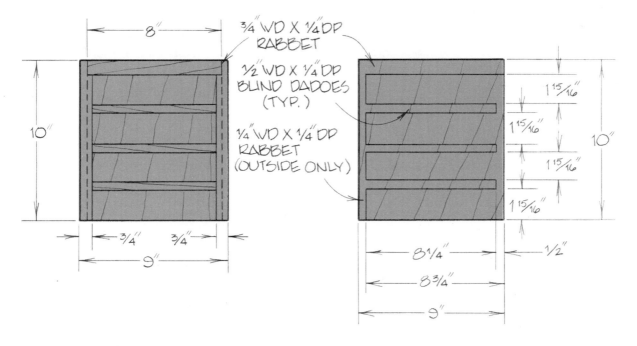

FRONT VIEW   **OUTER SIDE LAYOUT**

CABINET DRAWER UNIT

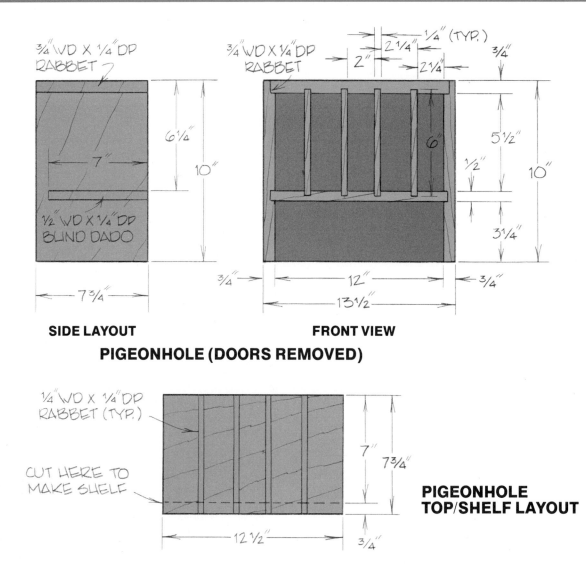

¾" WD X ¼" DP
RABBET

6¼"

7"

10"

½" WD X ¼" DP
BLIND DADO

7¾"

SIDE LAYOUT

¾" WD X ¼" DP
RABBET

¼" (TYP.)
2¼"
2"
2¼"

¾"

5½"

6"

½"

10"

3¼"

¾"   12"   ¾"

13½"

FRONT VIEW

PIGEONHOLE (DOORS REMOVED)

¼" WD X ¼" DP
RABBET (TYP.)

CUT HERE TO
MAKE SHELF

7"

7¾"

12½"

¾"

**PIGEONHOLE
TOP/SHELF LAYOUT**

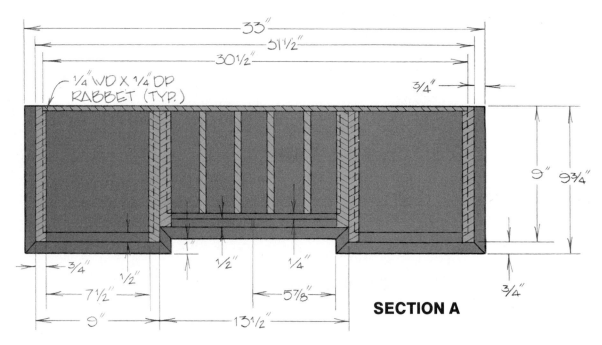

33"

31½"

30½"

¼" WD X ¼" DP
RABBET (TYP.)

¾"

9"   9¾"

1"

½"   ¼"

¾"   ½"

7½"

9"

5⅞"

13½"

¾"

SECTION A

13

Cut the shape of the cabinet bottom and pigeonhole dividers. The pigeonhole unit is not as deep as the drawer units. This gives the assembled cabinet a "blockfront" contour. The cabinet bottom is notched to accommodate this contour, as shown in *Section A.* Cut the notch with a saber saw or a band saw, and sand the sawed edges smooth.

Enlarge the *Pigeonhole Divider Pattern* and trace it onto the front edge of one divider. Stack the dividers and cut all four parts at once using a band saw, scroll saw, or saber saw. Cutting four at once eliminates layout work, and it ensures all the dividers will be uniform.

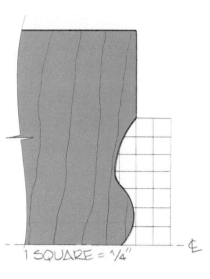

PIGEONHOLE DIVIDER PATTERN

1 SQUARE = 1/4"

14

Shape the edges of the cabinet top and bottom. With a shaper or a router, round over the side and front edges of the cabinet top and bottom, cutting the same profile as on the top and the drop leaf.

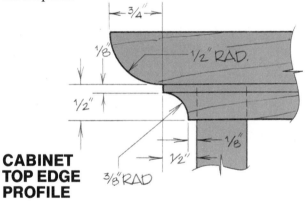

CABINET TOP EDGE PROFILE

To completely shape the bottom edge, you'll have to do a little hand carving inside the notched area. Router and shaper cutters will not completely cut an inside corner — their pilots prevent this. At these corners, finish rounding the edge with a carving chisel. (See Figure 5.)

5/Round the inside corners of the cabinet bottom with a carving chisel. Smooth the carved area with a file or a riffler, blending it into the machined edges.

15

Make the moldings. To make the moldings that are applied around the top of the cabinet, cut a 3⁄8"-radius cove in the edge of a 1⁄2"-thick board with your router or shaper. (For safety, the board should be as wide and as long as possible — no less than 4" x 18".) Rip the shaped edge free of the board on your table saw. (See Figure 6.) Repeat until you have made the moldings that you need.

6/To make small moldings, always cut the shape in a wide board, then rip the molding free. Never try to shape narrow stock because it may break up as you're machining it.

16

Assemble the cabinet. Finish sand all of the cabinet parts that you have made. Dry assemble the cabinet units. If the joints fit properly, reassemble each unit with glue. After the glue sets, drive 4d finishing nails through the tops and into the sides.

Next, glue the units together, side to side. Attach the top and the bottom to the assembly with flathead wood screws. Drive the screws through the bottom into the unit sides, and through the unit tops and into the cabinet top. Countersink the screw heads, but don't bother to cover them. You won't see them when the project is completed. Finally, attach the back, driving brads through it into the unit sides.

Apply molding around the sides and front of the cabinet, just under the top. Use miter joints wherever the molding pieces meet. Secure the moldings with glue and brads.

17

Make and fit the drawers. The drawer sides are joined to the front and back by rabbet and dado joints. The drawer bottom floats in a groove. Cut these grooves, dadoes, and rabbets with a router or a dado cutter.

Finish sand the drawer parts, then dry assemble them. If the fits are satisfactory, reassemble the fronts, backs, and sides with glue. Do *not* glue the bottoms in place; let them float in the grooves.

Lightly sand the joints to make them flush and clean. Attach the pulls, and test fit the drawers in the cabinet. If a drawer binds, plane a little stock off the area that seems to be sticking. When all of the drawers slide easily, rub the bottom edges with paraffin.

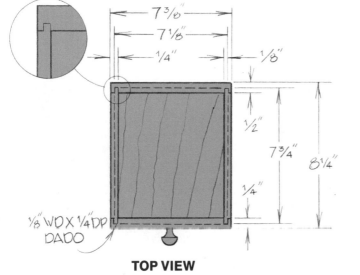

TOP VIEW

FRONT VIEW

CABINET DRAWER

18

Hinge the doors to the cabinet. Finish sand the doors and drill the bottom edges, near the inside corners, for bullet catches. (See Figure 7.) Cut the hinge mortises in the outside door edges and the inside edges of the pigeonhole sides. Install the doors with butt hinges. Attach the striker plates for the catches with wire nails. Depending on the make of the catch, you may have to mortise the cabinet bottom for the plates.

7/Bullet catches are easily installed on small doors. Drill a hole in the edge of the door to hold the barrel of the catch. When properly installed, only the ball-end should protrude.

Completing the Desk

19 **Attach the cabinet to the table.** Place the completed cabinet on the table. Hold it in place by driving two flathead wood screws through the table top into the cabinet bottom. Don't glue the assemblies together; the screws will be sufficient. It will be easy to take the desk apart should you need to move it or repair it.

20 **Apply a finish.** Remove all the drawers and all the hardware — pulls, hinges, and striker plates. Remove the cabinet from the table, and do any necessary touch-up sanding. Apply a finish to the project. Be certain to apply as many coats of finish to the underside of the table top and the inside of the cabinet as you do to the outside surfaces — this will help keep the assemblies from warping or distorting. Do *not,* however, finish the drawer assemblies other than the drawer fronts. Traditionally, the insides of drawers are left raw so that they will absorb moisture and odors from their contents. When the finish dries, reassemble the desk.

Step-by-Step: Making Lock Joints

For joining drawers, lock joints (sometimes called box joints) are an excellent alternative to traditional dovetails. The necessary cuts can be made on a table saw with a dado cutter.

Cut dadoes in the drawer sides. *Using the miter gauge to guide the ¾"-thick stock, cut a ¼"-wide, ⅜"-deep dado across each drawer side, ¼" from the front end. When making several drawers, clamp a stop block to the rip fence to automatically position the stock in the miter gauge.*

Cut the inner tongue to length. *Using the dado cutter as a saw blade, cut each inner tongue ⅜" long, leaving the outer tongues ¾" long. Guide the stock with the miter gauge.*

Cut tongues in the drawer faces. *Make ¼"-wide, ¾"-deep grooves in the butt ends of the drawer front, forming two ¼"-wide tongues in each end. Use the rip fence to guide the stock.*

Assemble the lock joints. *Glue the inner tongues on the drawer front into the dado in each drawer side. The outside face of each side should be flush with end of the outer tongues.*

Mantle Clock

The American mantle clock — a sawed-off version of the English grandfather clock — was an early triumph of Yankee ingenuity.

In the early nineteenth century, New England clockmakers experimented with new, mechanized metalworking and woodworking techniques, and, at the same time, a new, revolutionary method of production: the assembly line. The result was an outpouring of cheap-but-reliable small-case clocks. For most of the century, the New England states — particularly Massachusetts and Connecticut — exported mass-produced clocks to every corner of the globe. By mid-century, it was not uncommon to find American-made clocks sitting on cottage mantles in South America, Europe, and some parts of Asia.

Mantle clocks were even more popular here in the states, particularly among country folks. Not only were they inexpensive, they were simple enough to be mended by a blacksmith. Moreover, they required little space — and space was at a premium in country homes.

The clock shown was manufactured over 150 years ago by the Waterbury Clock Company in Connecticut. The construction is straightforward. The case is a box with applied moldings and a frame door. Traditional brass clockworks are mounted on a small shelf in the cabinet. The dimensions will also permit a modern quartz movement.

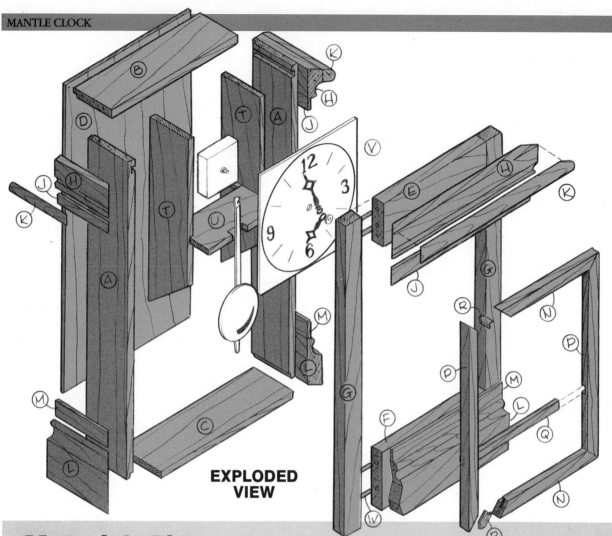

EXPLODED VIEW

Materials List

FINISHED DIMENSIONS

PARTS

A.	Sides (2)	¾" x 3" x 25½"
B.	Top	½" x 3" x 12"
C.	Bottom	½" x 2¾" x 12"
D.	Back	¼" x 12" x 24¾"
E.	Top face frame rail	1" x 3½" x 10"
F.	Bottom face frame rail	1" x 5¼" x 10"
G.	Face frame stiles (2)	1" x 1½" x 25½"
H.	Top panel molding (total)	¾" x 2¾" x 25"
J.	Top stop molding (total)	¼" x ¾" x 23"
K.	Top bead molding (total)	⅝" x 1" x 27"
L.	Bottom panel molding (total)	¾" x 4" x 25"
M.	Bottom stop molding (total)	¼" x 1¼" x 23"
N.	Top/bottom door rails (2)	⅝" x ⅞" x 9⅞"
P.	Door stiles (2)	⅝" x ⅞" x 16⅝"
Q.	Middle door rail	⅜" x ⅞" x 9⅞"
R.	Splines (4)	⅛" x 1" x 1⅝"
T.	Brackets (2)	½" x 2¼" x 15"
U.	Clockworks shelf	½" x 2¼" x 6½"
V.	Clock face*	¼" x 8½" x 8½"
W.	Dowels (6)	¼"-dia. x 2"

This piece may be eliminated if you use a metal or a ceramic clock face.

HARDWARE

Clockworks (either mechanical or electrical)
Pendulum and bob
Clock face (paper, metal, or ceramic)
4" Hour hand (approximate length)
3" Minute hand (approximate length)
1" x 1" Butt hinges and mounting screws (1 pair)
Small door pull
Bullet catch
#8 x 1" Roundhead wood screws and flat washers (8 sets)
#8 x 1" Flathead wood screws (8)
#8 x 1¼" Flathead wood screws (8)
#6 x ¾" Flathead wood screws (4)
1" Brads (20–24)
⅛" x 8⅝" x 8⅝" Glass pane
⅛" x 6⅛" x 8⅝" Glass pane
Glazing points (12–16)

1

Select the clockworks and establish the case dimensions. As noted, the case will accommodate either brass (mechanical) works or quartz (electrical) works. Similarly, it will accept clock face diameters from 8″ to 9″. An enormous number of choices result. You can select the chimes that will play, the lettering style on the face, even the look of the hands and the pendulum. (The clock shown in the drawings has a quartz movement, a 12″ plain pendulum, a face in the Regulator style, and black metal hands.) Here are two sources for clockmaking supplies:

Klockit
P.O. Box 629
Lake Geneva, WI 53147

Craft Products Company
Clintonville, WI 54929

Purchase the works and the face *before* you make the case. In addition to the physical dimensions of these parts, you'll also need to know how the works are mounted, and the length and the swing of the pendulum. Carefully measure the works and the face. Mount the works on a scrap board and set the pendulum in motion to measure the swing. Don't take the manufacturer's word for it; the swing of individual works can vary as much as 1″ from what the catalog advertises.

If necessary to accommodate the works and the face, alter the dimensions of the case. Remember, you not only

TRY THIS! Let the clockworks, mounted on the scrap board, run while you build the case. Clockworks — whether they are quartz or brass — are not adjusted at the factory. To adjust the works and the pendulum to keep accurate time, the clockworks must run several weeks. If you chose brass works, shroud them with a piece of tin or plastic so that they don't collect dust.

must make room for the clock parts, you must position the clock shaft (to which the hands are attached) directly in the center of the upper door panel (as shown in the *Front View*) and the pendulum bob must be visible through the lower door panel. Depending on how the works are mounted, you may have to reposition the clockworks shelf. Quartz movements are usually mounted on the back of the clock face. In this situation, the shelf should be positioned approximately 1″ *below* the works; don't eliminate it, for it stabilizes the brackets. Brass works are mounted on the shelf, so you have to position it so that the clock shaft is at the proper height. In each case, you must notch the shelf to provide clearance for the pendulum.

2

Cut the parts to size. With the case configuration set, select the stock. Stability is crucial in a pendulum clock, even one with a quartz movement. Choose clear, tightly-grained wood. Most of the old clock cases were made from cherry, walnut, and hard maple. A few were made from white pine and grain-painted to look like mahogany.

For the case shown, you'll need approximately 2½ board feet of 6/4 or 8/4 lumber, 8 board feet of 4/4 lumber, and a quarter-sheet (2′ x 4′) of ¼″ cabinet-grade plywood. To make the face frame, top bead mold-

ing, and splines, plane the thicker stock to 1″ thick. Of the 4/4 stock, plane 3 board feet to ¾″ thick for the sides and the panel moldings, 2 board feet to ⅝″ thick for the door frame, 2 board feet to ½″ thick for the top, bottom, brackets, and clockworks shelf, ½ board foot to ⅜″ thick for the middle door frame rail, and 1 board foot to ¼″ thick for the stop moldings. Use plywood for the back and face. Cut all the parts, except the bead molding and splines. Cut the splines ¼″-½″ longer than specified, and don't cut the bead molding at all. Miter the ends of the top and bottom door rails and the door stiles at 45°.

3

Machine the case parts. The case is joined with dadoes and rabbets. Cut them using a router or a dado cutter. Here's a list:

- ½″-wide x ¼″-deep dadoes in the sides for the top
- ½″-wide x ¼″-deep dadoes in the brackets for the clockworks shelf
- ½″-wide x ¼″-deep rabbets in the sides for the bottom

- ¼″-wide x ¼″-deep rabbets in the back edge of the sides for the back

While you're set up to make dadoes and rabbets, also cut the ⅞″-wide, ⅜″-deep dadoes in the door stiles for the middle rail. In addition, cut a notch in the clockworks shelf for the pendulum. Back up the shelf with scrap to prevent the dado cutter from tearing the stock.

4

Make the face frame. Dowel the members of the face frame together. Use a doweling jig as a guide to drill the holes in the frame members. Glue the stiles to the rails, making sure the frame is square when you clamp it.

5

Assemble the case. Finish sand the case parts, without breaking edges or corners that join other parts. Assemble the sides, top, and bottom with glue and #8 x 1¼″ flathead wood screws. Glue the face frame to the front of the case. Clamp the back in place to keep the assembly square, but do *not* fasten it yet. You can, however, fasten the brackets and the shelf to the back with #8 x 1″ flathead wood screws.

Important: If you are using a quartz movement, or a movement that mounts on the back of the clock face, glue the clockworks shelf to the brackets. If your movement mounts on the shelf, just slide the shelf into the dadoes, so it (and the works) can be removed easily for maintenance and repairs. (To remove the shelf, loosen the screws that hold it to the back and pull it out.)

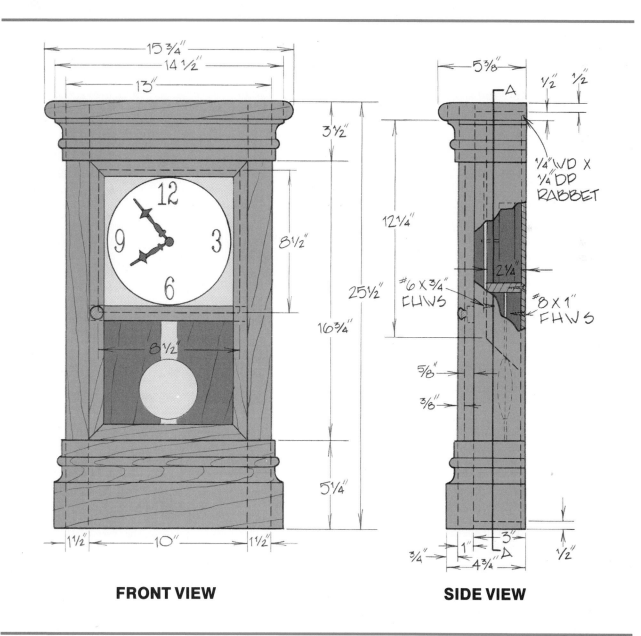

FRONT VIEW

SIDE VIEW

6

Make the molding. The stop molding is a rectangular strip and does not require any shaping. The other two — the panel moldings and the bead molding — must be shaped with a table-mounted router, shaper, or molding head in a table saw. Each of these shapes requires multiple passes to create them.

To make the panel molding with a shaper or molder, first cut the ¼″-radius bead shape with a nosing cutter. (You can also use a quarter-round cutter, but you must make an extra pass.) Cut some scraps to test the cutter alignment for the next step. When the alignment is correct, make the ½″-radius cove using a cove cutter. (See Figure 1.)

If you use a router, you won't be able to make the panel molding precisely as it's shown. The dimensions of the beads and coves will change slightly because of bits available. Make the bead shape in two passes with a point-cutting quarter-round bit. Cut the cove with a core-box bit. Create the flat area between the bead and the cove with a ¾″ straight bit. (See Figure 2.)

The procedure for making the bead molding is the same, whether you use a router, shaper, or molder. Make two passes with a ½″-radius quarter-round bit or cutter. Cut one edge of a wide board, turn the board over, then cut the other to complete the bead shape. Rip the bead free of the stock on a table saw. (See Figure 3.)

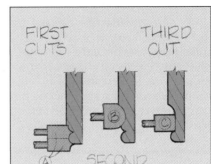

2/If you have a router, use a point-cutting quarter-round bit (a), followed by a core-box bit (b), then a ¾″ straight bit (c) to create the panel molding.

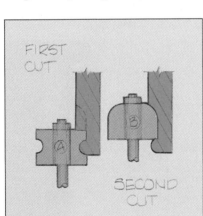

1/If you have a shaper or molder, use a nosing cutter (a), followed by a cove cutter (b), to create the panel molding shape. Since these cutters are usually 1″ high, the cuts will overlap.

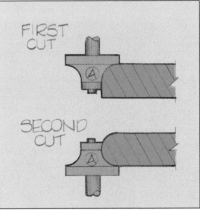

3/To shape the bead molding, make two passes with a quarter-round bit or cutter (a).

7

Apply the moldings to the case. Finish sand the moldings and glue them together, edge to edge and face to face, as shown in the *Top Molding Detail* and *Bottom Molding Detail.* Cut the built-up moldings to size, mitering the ends where they will join. Glue the front moldings to the case. Glue *just the mitered end and the first 1″* of each side molding to the case. Secure the other end with a #8 x 1″ roundhead wood screw and flat washer, as shown in *Section A.* The grain of the side moldings opposes the grain of the sides, and a glue joint will split if the side moldings are glued along their full length. Drill oversized shank holes in the sides (but not in the moldings) so that the sides can expand and contract.

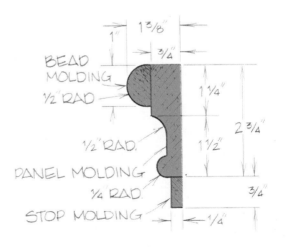

TOP MOLDING DETAIL

8

Assemble the door.   The door frame is held together with splines, as shown in the *Door Frame Joinery Detail*. Cut the spline slots in the mitered ends of the frame members on a table saw. (See Figure 4.) Assemble the frame with glue, making sure it is square before you apply the clamps.

After the glue dries, file and sand the ends of the splines flush with the surface of the door frame. With a router and a piloted rabbeting bit, cut a ¼″-wide, ¼″-deep rabbet around the inside edge of *both* the top and bottom door frame openings. Square the corners of the rabbets with a hand chisel. These rabbets will hold the glass panels.

4/*Use an ordinary combination blade to cut the ⅛″-wide slots for the splines. A tenoning jig holds the frame member at the proper angle to the blade.*

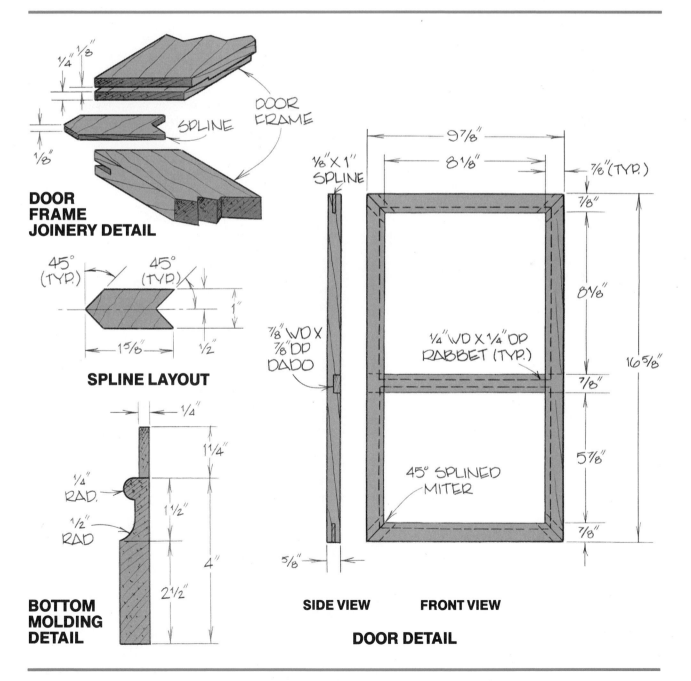

DOOR FRAME JOINERY DETAIL

SPLINE LAYOUT

BOTTOM MOLDING DETAIL

SIDE VIEW   **FRONT VIEW**

DOOR DETAIL

9 **Mount the door.** Fit the door to the case. There should be a $1/16''$ gap between the door and face frames, all around the perimeter of the door. Plane or file the door as necessary to achieve the proper fit. Cut hinge mortises in the door and face frames, then mount the door. Install a catch and a pull.

TRY THIS! To get a perfect fit, make the door *slightly* larger than you need, then plane it down to fit the case.

10 **Install the back.** Attach the back to the case with brads. Do *not* glue it. To access the works for maintenance and repair, you must be able to remove the back.

11 **Install the works and face.** Glue the paper face to the clock face board (unless you have purchased a metal or ceramic face). Drill a hole for the clock shaft. If you are using a quartz movement, mount it on the back of the face board. If you are using a brass movement, mount it on the clockworks shelf.

Position the face in the case, attaching it to the brackets with #6 x ¾″ brass flathead wood screws. Countersink these screws, but do *not* cover the heads. Future maintenance and repair may necessitate removal of the clock face. Finally, install the hands and pendulum.

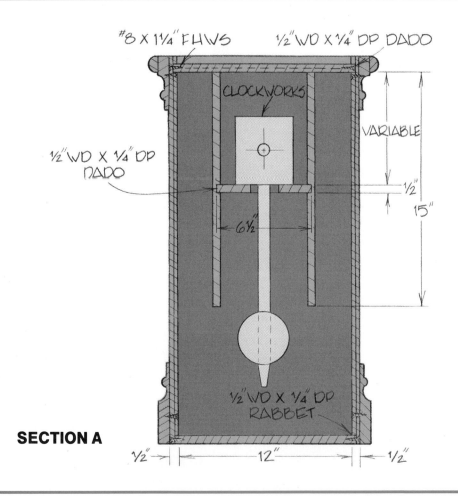

SECTION A

12 **Finish the completed case.** When you are certain that the works and face fit properly and that the pendulum has room to swing, disassemble the clock. Remove the works and the face. Take the door from its hinges, and remove all hardware. Do any touch-up sanding necessary and apply a finish. After the finish dries, reassemble the clock.

13 **Install the glass door panels.** Most country clocks had a design painted on the glass door panels. While not essential, the design does serve an important aesthetic purpose. It allows you to see the face and swinging bob, while hiding the clock face mounting screws, the brackets, and the unadorned interior of the case.

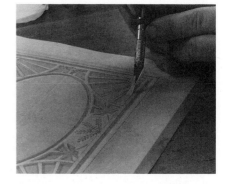

5/To apply the designs on the glass door panels, you'll need masking film, which is available at craft or hobby shops.

Glass painting is a fine art that cannot be adequately explained in a few paragraphs. To make a traditional glass painting for your clock, consult books on the subject at your library. Otherwise, the design can be applied in a much simpler manner.

Purchase self-stick frosted masking film (sometimes called frisket material) at a craft or hobby store. Apply the film to the glass. Enlarge the *Upper Door Pattern* and *Lower Door Pattern* and trace them onto the film. Cut the patterns, using a razor blade or a very sharp knife, and peel away the areas to be painted. (See Figure 5.)

Spray the masked side of the glass with enamel paint. Apply 2-3 coats, letting it dry between each coat. Remove the remaining masking film *except* for the film covering the inner circle (upper panel) and oval (lower panel).

As you work, carefully separate the film from the paint so that the paint doesn't peel up, too. Spray the glass with several coats of a *contrasting* color. Let it dry, then peel up all the masking film. The perimeter of each glass panel should be painted with a two-color design, but the interior should be clear, allowing you to view the clock face and the bob.

Clean the glass with window cleaner. Using glazing points, secure the panels in the door frame with the painted sides facing in. Cover the faces of the glazing points with masking tape to avoid scratching the paint.

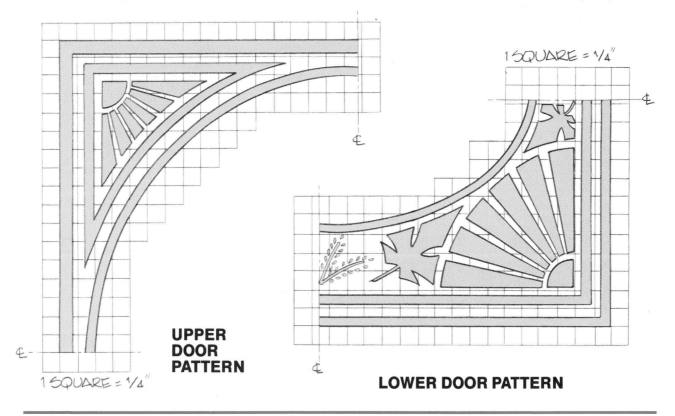

1 SQUARE = ¼"

UPPER DOOR PATTERN

1 SQUARE = ¼"

LOWER DOOR PATTERN

Pipebox

Although we think of these small, hanging boxes as "pipeboxes," they were rarely used to hold pipes. Most country gents only had one or two pipes — hardly enough to fill a pipebox — and those had short stems. Only in taverns and inns, where the proprietor kept a selection of long-stem clay pipes for guests, were pipeboxes used to hold pipes.

These boxes had another purpose altogether — and another name. They were originally intended to hold candles, though not the wax candles we think of — these are best stored lying down in a cool place. Rather, the boxes held slender sticks of candlewood (resinous pine) or lengths of dried, pithy rush saturated with tallow. Wax candles were a luxury in colonial America; country folks commonly burned these strips of pine and rush for light at night. Because they burned fairly quickly, a large supply had to be kept on hand, hence the candleboxes.

The box shown here is typical of early American candleboxes — or pipeboxes, if you prefer. A deep bin, open at the top, held the candlewood or the rush. The small drawer at the bottom held fire-making supplies: pieces of flint, an iron striker, and tinder.

Materials List

FINISHED DIMENSIONS

PARTS

A.	Back	½" x 5" x 16½"
B.	Sides (2)	½" x 4½" x 12½"
C.	Front	½" x 4" x 9½"
D.	Bin bottom	½" x 4" x 4"
E.	Bottom	½" x 5" x 5½"
F.	Drawer front	½" x 1⅞" x 3⅞"
G.	Drawer sides (2)	¼" x 1⅝" x 4¼"
H.	Drawer back	¼" x 1⅝" x 3⅜"
J.	Drawer bottom	¼" x 3⅞" x 4¼"
K.	Drawer pull	¾" dia. x 1¼"

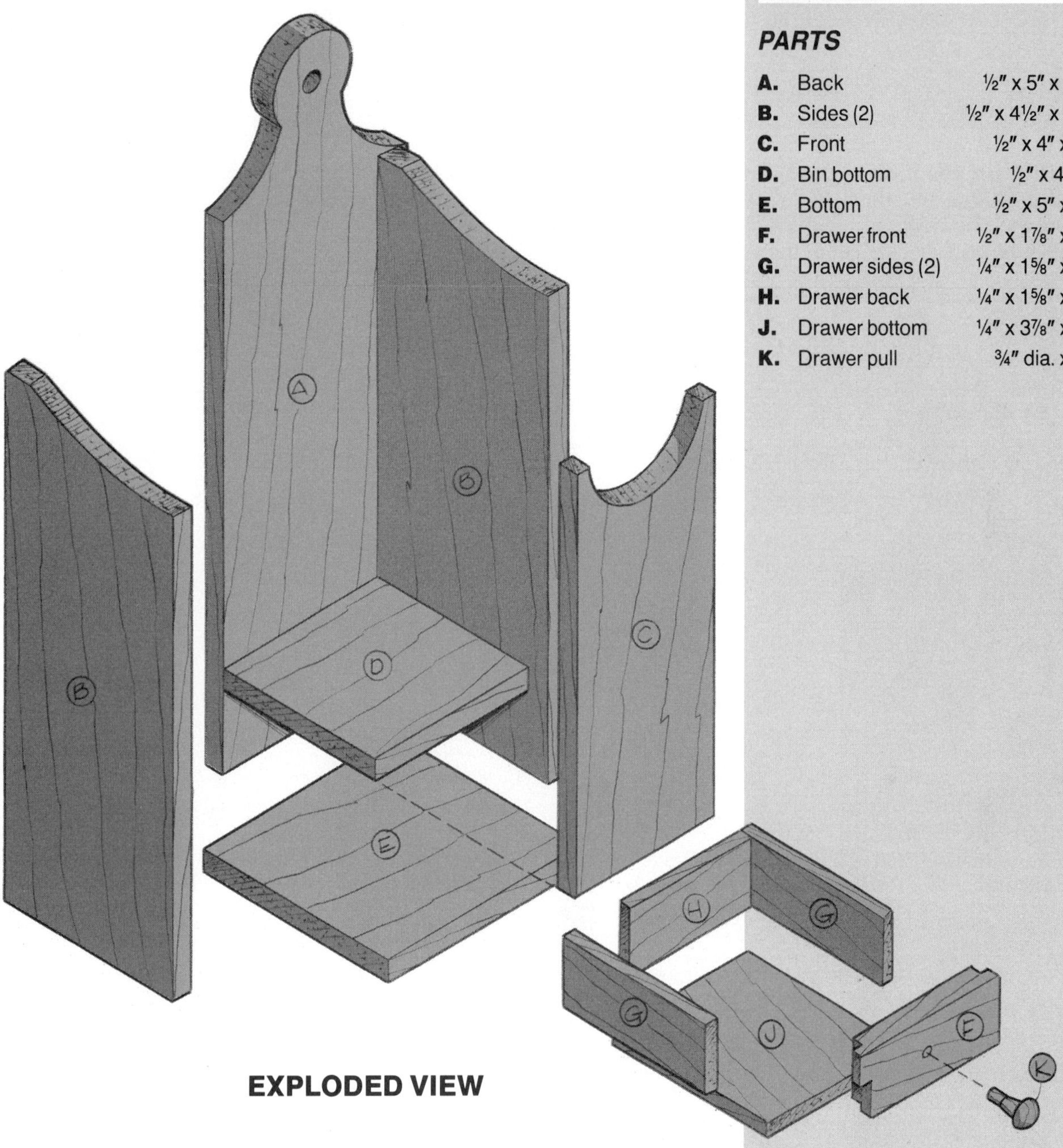

HARDWARE

1" Brads (20–24)
¾" Brads (12–16)

EXPLODED VIEW

1 **Cut all parts to size.** This project can be made with less than 2½ board feet of lumber — you may want to use scrap wood left over from a larger project. Plane approximately 2 board feet ½″ thick, and the remainder to ¼″ thick. Then cut the parts to the sizes shown in the Materials List.

2 **Cut out the sides, back, and front.** Lay out the front and the sides, as shown in the *Front View* and the *Side View*. Enlarge the *Back Pattern* and trace it on the back stock. Cut out the shapes of these parts with a band saw, saber saw, or scroll saw. Drill a ½″-diameter hole through the back, where shown in the *Front View*.

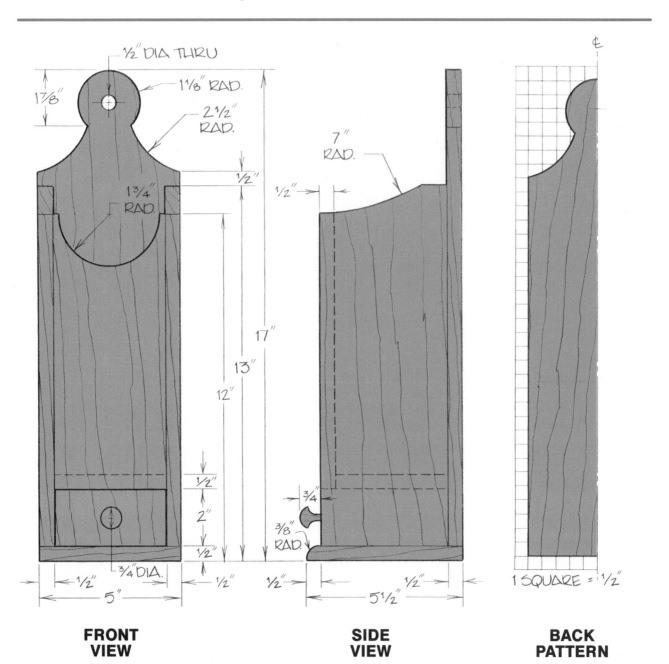

FRONT VIEW

SIDE VIEW

BACK PATTERN

3
Shape the edge of the bottom. With a router or a shaper, round over the front edge of the bottom, as shown in the *Side View.* You can also use a block plane, making repeated passes until the edge is properly rounded. (See Figure 1.)

1/Sometimes it's faster to do things by hand. In half the time it takes you to set up a router, you can round over the front edge of the bottom with a hand plane.

4
Assemble the pipebox. Finish sand the parts of the pipebox, being careful not to round over any adjoining corners or edges. Assemble the box using glue and brads. Attach the bin bottom to the front first. Then attach the sides, then the back. Finally, attach the bottom to the pipebox assembly. Set the brads, and cover the heads with wood putty.

TRY THIS! When assembling the parts of the pipebox, drive the brads at an angle. Alternate the angles, so that you drive the first brad tilted toward the right, the next one toward the left, and so on. This will hold the parts together more securely.

BRADS

5
Build the drawer. With a router or table saw, cut three ¼″-wide, ¼″-deep rabbets in the drawer front. Make one rabbet along the bottom, and one across each end. Then drill a ¼″-diameter hole through the drawer front, centered in the face of the stock.

Finish sand the parts of the drawer. Assemble the drawer with glue and brads, fitting the sides to the drawer front first, then adding the back and the bottom.

Turn a drawer pull to the profile shown in the *Drawer Pull Detail.* If you don't have a lathe, you can use your drill press to make small turnings. (See Figures 2 and 3.) Glue the drawer pull into the hole in the drawer front.

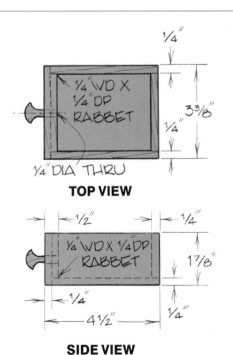

¼″

¼″ WD X ¼″ DP RABBET

3⅜″

¼″

¼″ DIA THRU

TOP VIEW

½″   ¼″

¼″ WD X ¼″ DP RABBET

1⅞″

¼″

4½″

¼″

DRAWER

SIDE VIEW

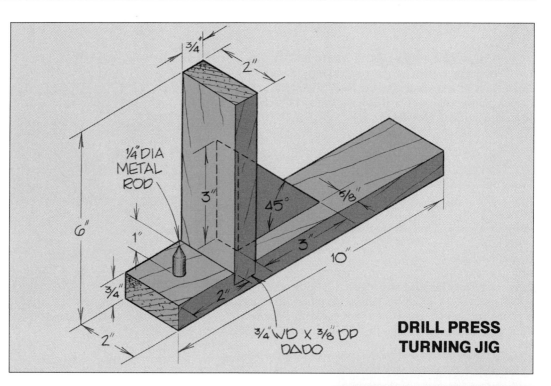

DRILL PRESS TURNING JIG

2/This simple jig will enable you to create small turnings on a drill press. Clamp the top end of the stock in the chuck, and use a nail as a pivot for the bottom end. A removable dowel serves as a tool rest.

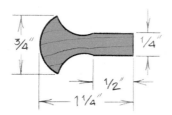

DRAWER PULL DETAIL

3/If the stock is too large to hold in the drill press chuck, drive a #12 x 1¼" roundhead wood screw into the top end of the stock, leaving the shank exposed. Cut the head off the screw, and clamp the shank in the chuck. After you complete the turning, remove the screw with a pair of pliers.

6 **Fit the drawer to the pipebox.**   Sand the drawer joints to clean them up and make all the surfaces flush. Then fit the drawer to the pipebox. If it binds, remove a little stock with a sander or a plane.

TRY THIS!   For a perfect fit, make the drawer slightly oversized. Carefully sand it to its final dimensions, testing the fit in the pipebox as you sand.

7 **Finish the pipebox.**   Do any necessary touch-up sanding, then apply a finish to the completed project. If you use a finish that builds up on the surface, such as paint or varnish, do not apply it to the sides or bottom of a closely fitted drawer, or to the inside of the drawer cavity. These surfaces should be covered with a penetrating finish. The pipebox shown here is painted, but the drawer sides, bottom, and cavity are finished with tung oil.

Fretwork Mirror

Country folk often referred to mirrors as "lights." If a room had few windows and was poorly lighted, mirrors were hung in strategic places. They caught the sunlight and reflected it into the corners.

Mirrors were framed many ways, but one of the most popular was the fretwork frame shown here. The intricate fretwork shapes were copied from stylized cloud forms used by Japanese artists and craftsmen. English cabinetmakers first saw them on furniture imported from the orient in the mid-1700s. The cloud forms caught on, and American craftsmen were soon copying their English counterparts. As the style spread, fretwork mirrors appeared in the American cities first, then in towns, and finally in the country.

Although the frame looks complex, it is simple to make. The basic frame is made like a picture frame, using ordinary miter joints. The fretwork is cut from thin stock, then glued into grooves in the frame.

Materials List

FINISHED DIMENSIONS

PARTS

A. Horizontal stretchers (2) — ¾" x 1½" x 16½"

B. Vertical stretchers (2) — ¾" x 1½" x 27"

C. Top fretwork — ¼" x 8" x 17¼"

D. Bottom fretwork — ¼" x 5" x 17¼"

E. Top side fretwork (2) — ¼" x 3½" x 10⅞"

F. Bottom side fretwork (2) — ¼" x 3⅜" x 7½"

G. Splines (4) — ⅛" x 1" x 2¼"

H. Mirror back — ¼" x 14¼" x 24¾"

HARDWARE

⅛" x 14¼" x 24¾" Mirror
¾" Brads (8–12)
¼" Eye screws (2)
30# Picture hanging wire (18")

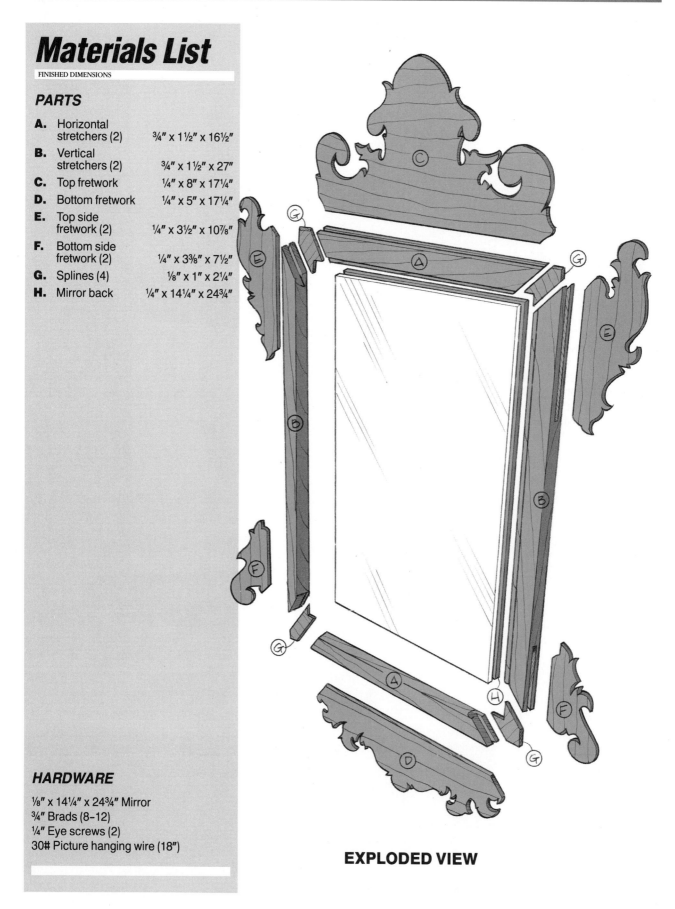

EXPLODED VIEW

1 Determine the size of the mirror.

Determine the size of the mirror. The fretwork mirror can be made any size that you want, as long as you maintain the *proportions*. At an overall size of 22½″ by 39″, our mirror is fairly large, especially for a country mirror. You may want to make it only two-thirds or one-half of the size shown here. To do this, simply divide the length of the stretchers and the scale of the patterns by the appropriate number (1½ to reduce the dimensions to two-thirds, or 2 to reduce them to one-half). The stretchers on a two-thirds-scale mirror, for example, would be 18″ and 11″ long. When you enlarge the patterns, each square would be equal to ⅓″ rather than ½″. *All other dimensions*

remain the same. The stretchers must be ¾″ thick and 1½″ wide, no matter what their length. The fretwork must be ¼″ thick.

The only other adjustment necessary is to the size of the fretwork tongues and the grooves they fit into. As the size of the fretwork is reduced, the width of the portion that fits into the groove — the tongue — shrinks proportionately. You must adjust the pattern to maintain the ½″ width of the tongue, regardless of the size of the fretwork. Though the depth of the groove remains at ½″ in any case, you must adjust the length to accommodate the actual length of the tongue.

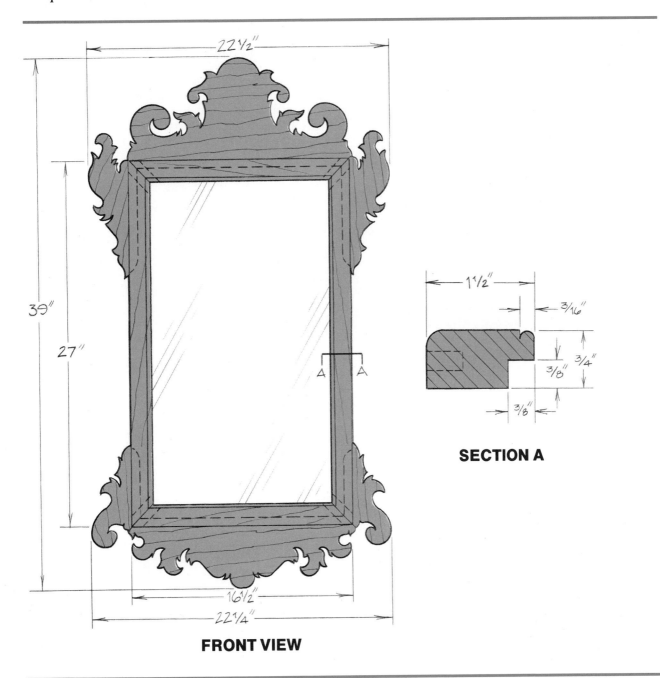

SECTION A

FRONT VIEW

2 Select and prepare the stock.

Decide on the type of wood you want to use. Most country fretwork mirrors were made from maple, cherry, or walnut. Their city cousins were made from imported mahogany.

Determine how much wood you need. As shown, the frame can be made from approximately 4 board feet of stock. (Smaller mirrors will, of course, require less stock.) Select a 4/4 (four-quarters) board, 11¼″ wide or more, and 48″ long. Rip two 1½″-wide strips. Then resaw the remainder on your band saw to get two boards of equal thickness and about 8″ wide and 48″ long.

Plane the 1½″-wide strips to ¾″ thick, and the resawed boards to ¼″ thick. Cut a 12″ length of the ¼″-thick material and plane it to ⅛″ thick. Use the ¾″ stock to make the stretchers, the ¼″ stock for the fretwork, and the ⅛″ stock for the splines. To make the mirror back, you'll need a quarter sheet (2′ x 4′) of ¼″-thick hardboard.

3 Shape the stretchers.

The stretchers have a small, decorative bead on the front face, and a rabbet in the back to hold the mirror and mirror back. You can make both on a table saw, using a molding head to cut the bead and a dado cutter to cut the rabbet.

Cut the bead first. Insert a set of beading knives in the molding head, then mount the head on the saw arbor. Cut a single bead in the face of the stretcher stock, at what will be the inside edge. (See Figure 1.) Replace the molding head with a dado cutter, and cut a ⅜″-wide, ⅜″-deep rabbet in the back of the stretcher stock. (See Figure 2.)

Alternative method: You can use a router to make both the bead and the rabbet. Use a straight bit to cut the rabbet and a point-cut quarter-round bit to form the bead. (It will take two passes to make the bead —the bit cuts half of bead with each pass.)

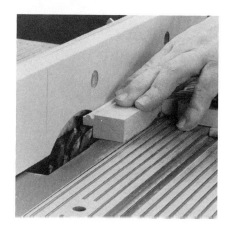

1/Beading knives will usually cut one, two, or three beads in one pass, depending on the position of the table saw's rip fence. With a wooden facing attached to the fence to protect the knives, set the fence to overlap the molding head enough that only one bead is cut.

2/Use a dado cutter to create the rabbet in the back of the stretcher stock. As you did when you made the bead, position the fence so that it overlaps the unused portion of the cutter. This helps protect your fingers and hands.

4 Miter and assemble the stretchers.

Finish sand the front face of the stretcher stock, smoothing the bead that you have just made. Then cut the stretchers to length, mitering the ends at 45°.

TRY THIS! To test whether the miter gauge is set to a perfect 45° angle, first make a small frame (3″–4″ to a side) of scrap wood and assemble it. If the miter joints gap at the *inside,* the angle is *greater* than 45° and needs to be reduced. If the joints gap at the *outside,* the angle is *less* than 45° and must be increased.

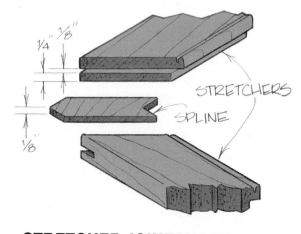

STRETCHERS
SPLINE

STRETCHER JOINERY DETAIL

After you miter the stretchers, cut ⅛"-wide, ½"-deep grooves in the mitered ends for splines. These grooves must be ¼" from the *back* face of the stretchers, as shown in the *Stretcher Joinery Detail,* so the splines won't be visible from the front. Cut the grooves on a table saw, using a combination blade. (See Figure 3.) Press the mitered surface of the stock to the saw table as you cut.

3/A combination blade will leave a ⅛"-wide kerf; it is the perfect tool for cutting spline grooves.

From the ⅛" stock, cut four splines. The grain *must* run side-to-side, as shown in the *Spline Layout,* so it crosses the joint, reinforcing it. If the grain runs end-to-end, it will parallel the joint and the spline will offer no reinforcement.

Warning: It's essential that you reinforce the miter joints with splines. The frame must be machined after it's assembled. Without the splines, the miter joints may come apart.

Dry assemble the stretchers and the splines to test the fit. Adjust the size of the splines, if necessary — you should have plenty of ⅛" stock for new splines, if you need them. When the parts fit properly, assemble the frame with glue.

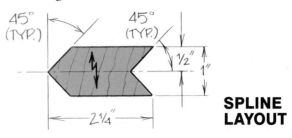

SPLINE LAYOUT

5 **Cut the fretwork.**   Enlarge the *Fretwork Patterns* and trace them on ¼" stock. Cut the shapes with a scroll saw fitted with a fine-cut blade. The job will take longer and you may break several blades, but fine-cut blades leave very smooth cuts. It will take a great deal less effort to remove the saw marks from the

cut edges. **Hint:** Use very light pressure when feeding the stock. This will save the blade.

Cut the mitered corners of the fretwork a little large — stay to the outside of the line with the saw blade. When it comes time to attach the fretwork to the frame, you can sand or file these corners down to get a perfect fit.

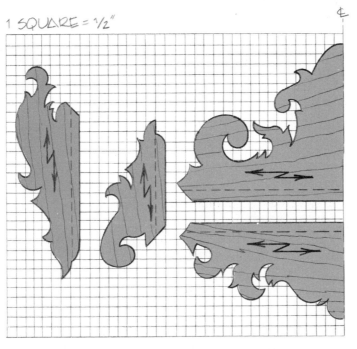

1 SQUARE = ½"

FRETWORK PATTERNS

6

Cut the fretwork grooves in the frame.
Lightly sand the frame's joints flush and clean. Set up the table saw with a dado cutter to plow grooves, ¼" wide and ½" deep, centered in the edge of the frame. The groove must be centered in the edge — precisely the same distance from both the back and the front faces. Cut test grooves in scraps as you refine the setup. When you're satisfied the setup is right, cut the grooves in the top and bottom stretchers.

Next, clamp a block to the rip fence to stop the cut, and cut the blind grooves in the top of the side stretchers. Readjust the position of the stop block and cut the blind grooves in the bottom of the side stretchers. (See Figure 4.)

Alternative method: The grooves can be cut using a ¼" straight bit and a table-mounted router.

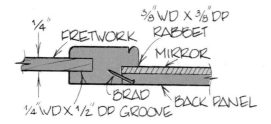

FRETWORK JOINERY DETAIL

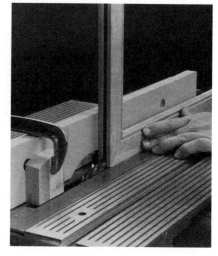

*4/Because the frame must be flopped back-to-front several times as you work, the fence must be positioned so the dado cutter plows the groove **precisely** in the center of the stock. If the grooves aren't centered, they won't meet properly at the corners.*

7

Glue the fretwork to the stretchers.
Finish sand the frame and fretwork. Then test-fit the fretwork in the grooves. Using a disk sander or a flat file, true up the fretwork's mitered corners. You may also have to fit the rounded edge of the side fretwork pieces to the blind ends of the grooves. When all the fretwork pieces fit properly, glue them in place.

8

Finish the completed frame. Do any touch-up sanding necessary and apply a finish. Traditionally, country craftsmen used a clear penetrating finish such as linseed oil or beeswax on these mirror frames. (They were rarely painted.) The frame shown is finished with tung oil.

9

Install the mirror. Lay the mirror in place and fit the back over it. Secure the mirror and back in the frame with small brads. Install eye screws in the side stretchers, one on either side, several inches from the top of the frame. Run 30# picture-hanging wire between the eyes, then hang the completed mirror as you would a picture frame.

Tilt-Top Candlestand

Because country homes were small, the people who lived in them seized every opportunity to conserve space. Some furniture was made to knock down or fold up when it wasn't being used. Other pieces were made to do double duty. The tilt-top candlestand is a good example of *both* of these practices.

When this small table wasn't needed, its top tilted to a vertical position so it could be stored against a wall, out of the way. Moreover, with the top in the vertical position, the candlestand could be used as a fire screen. The country cook had to keep a cooking fire going all year round. On a hot summer day, the tipped-up candlestand top shielded the cook and other people in the kitchen area from the fire's heat. In the winter, the top reflected heat into cold corners.

The tilt-top candlestand shown is typical of many older pieces. The top is a bit fancier than most, but you can substitute a round, oval, or rectangular top. The tilting top is mounted on a central post, and this is supported by three legs. Having three legs instead of four reduces the weight of the piece, and makes it easier to move around. It also keeps the table from wobbling. The floors of country homes were often uneven, and a three-legged table always sits solidly, whether the floor is even or not.

Materials List

FINISHED DIMENSIONS

PARTS

A.	Top	¾″ x 14″ x 22″
B.	Pivot block	1½″ x 6″ x 6″
C.	Braces (2)	¾″ x 1½″ x 14″
D.	Post	2¾″ dia. x 19″
E.	Legs (3)	¾″ x 4¼″ x 13¼″
F.	Wedge	⁷⁄₃₂″ x 1⅜″ x 1½″
G.	Dowels (6)	¼″ dia. x 1″
H.	Locking pin	½″ dia. x 2″

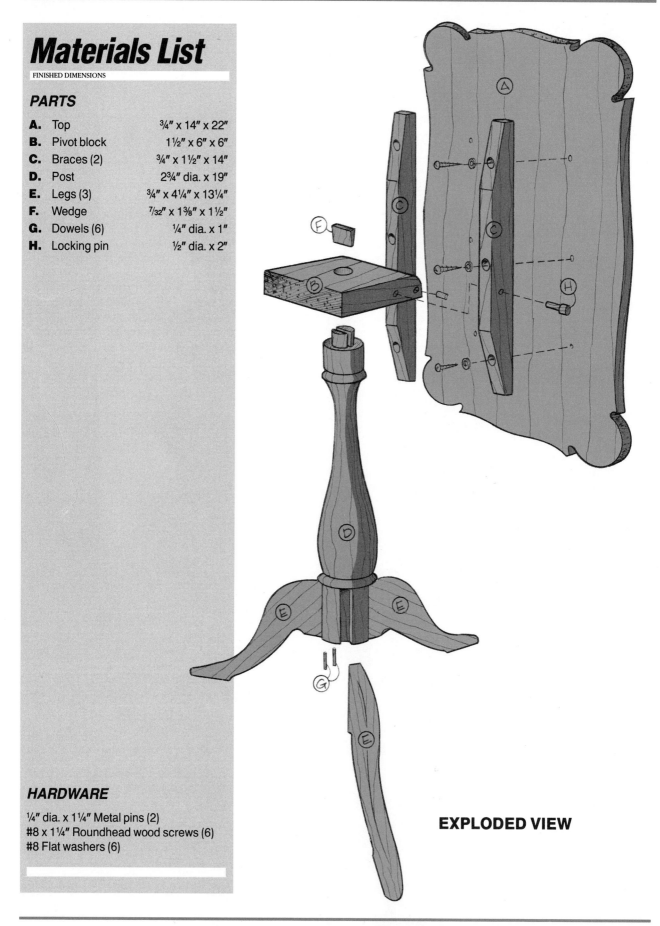

HARDWARE

¼″ dia. x 1¼″ Metal pins (2)
#8 x 1¼″ Roundhead wood screws (6)
#8 Flat washers (6)

EXPLODED VIEW

1

Cut the parts to size. Select attractive stock for the candlestand. It presents an excellent opportunity to use figured woods, or to combine different species. The candlestand shown has a curly maple top; the other parts are curly cherry. Other traditional combinations include walnut and maple, and walnut and cherry.

To make this project, you need approximately 5 board feet of 4/4 (four quarters) stock and a 3″ x 3″ turning square at least 20″ long. Plane most of the 4/4 stock to ¾″ thick, except for the stock that you will use to make the candlestand legs. Plane this 1/64″-1/32″ thicker — you'll see why later on in the project. Glue two pieces of ¾″ stock face to face to make a 1½″-thick piece for the pivot block. If necessary, glue up wide stock to make the top. Then cut the braces and the pivot block to the sizes specified in the Materials List.

2

Make the legs. Enlarge the *Leg Pattern* and trace it onto the leg stock. Cut out the legs with a band saw or a saber saw. Sand the sawed edges to remove the saw marks.

> **TRY THIS!** When you lay out each leg, it is crucial that the foot be at a right angle to the edge that joins to the post. Use a carpenter's square to check your layout *before* you cut out the legs.

Round the *top* edge of the legs — and only the top edge — with a shaper or a router, using a ⅜″-radius quarter-round bit. Scrape or file them to remove mill marks, then finish sand the legs.

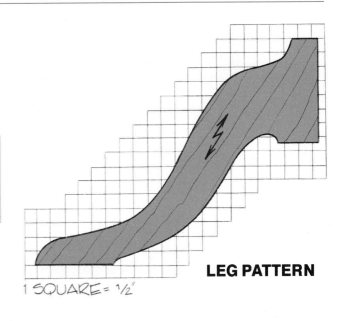

LEG PATTERN

1 SQUARE = ½″

3

Cut and shape the top. Make the top in a manner similar to the legs. Enlarge the top pattern from the *Top View*, and trace it on the stock. Drill ⅝″-diameter holes near each corner, as shown on the pattern. Then cut the shape with a band saw or saber saw. Sand the sawed edges and round them with a router and a ⅜″-radius quarter-round bit. Finish sand both the topside and the underside.

4

Make the braces. Taper the ends of the braces, as shown in the *Side View,* and sand the sawed edges. Mark the positions of the mounting screws, as shown in the *Top View.* Drill ⅜″-diameter, ¾″-deep counterbores and 3/16″ shank holes for each screw. The oversize shank holes allow the top to expand and contract.

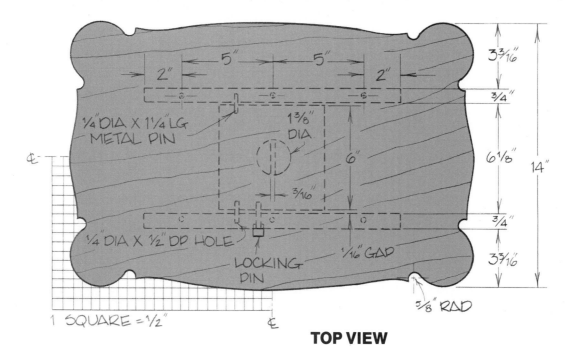

TOP VIEW

¾" DIA X 1¼" LG
METAL PIN

1⅜"
DIA

³⁄₁₆"

¼" DIA X ½" DP HOLE

LOCKING
PIN

1 SQUARE = ½"

3³⁄₁₆"

¾"

6⅛"   14"

¾"

3³⁄₁₆"

6"

¹⁄₁₆" GAP

⅝" RAD

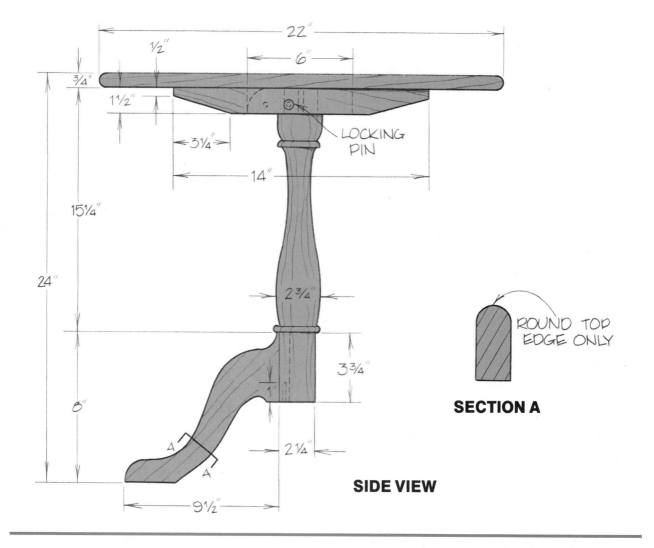

SIDE VIEW

22"

½"

¾"

6"

1½"

LOCKING
PIN

3¼"

14"

15¼"

24"

2¾"

3¾"

1"

8"

2¼"

9½"

ROUND TOP
EDGE ONLY

SECTION A

5

Make the pivots and the pivot blocks.
Drill a 1⅜″-diameter hole through the pivot
block so that you can mount it on the post. Mark the
pivot hole locations and the edge to be rounded off, as
shown in the *Pivot Block Detail*. Drill the ¼″-diameter,
¾″-deep pivot holes. Then cut the edge on your band
saw, with the block set on one side. File the rounded
edge smooth, then finish sand the block and the braces.

Turn the top upside down on your workbench. Lay
out the positions of the pivot block and braces on it. Put
dowel centers in the pivot block's pivot holes, set it in
place, and press the braces against it. The centers will
create small indentations on the braces. Drill a ¼″-diam-
eter, ½″-deep hole at each indentation.

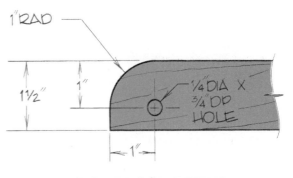

PIVOT BLOCK DETAIL

6

Turn and groove the post.
The legs of
the candlestand fit into grooves cut in the post.
Pieces of dowel are used as keys to hold the legs in
grooves, as shown in the *Foot-to-Post Joinery Detail*. This
joint is just as strong as a sliding dovetail, which was traditionally used on such candlestands, but it is much easier
to make.

Turn the post in *two* stages. In the first, turn the stock
to make a cylinder. In the second — after the grooves
have been routed — complete the profile of the post.

Start by cutting the post stock at least 1″ longer than
specified in the Materials List. Mount the stock on your
lathe and turn a cylinder, as straight as you can make it,
2¾″ in diameter. Lay out the beads, coves, and other
elements of the post profile, leaving at least ½″ of extra
stock at each end of the post. Turn *just* the lower portion
of the post — where the legs will be mounted — down
to 2¼″ in diameter. Finish sand this portion, including
the shoulder where the diameter changes. *Do not work
any other portion of the post.*

Remove the stock from the lathe. Lay out the grooves.
Each should be 120° from the last. Secure the post in a
V-jig. If you don't have one, make the V-jig as shown in
the *V-Jig Detail*.

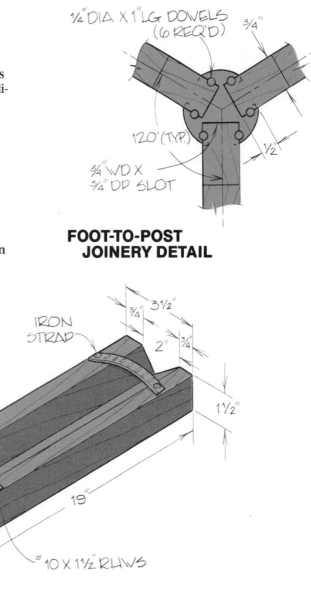

**FOOT-TO-POST
JOINERY DETAIL**

V-JIG DETAIL

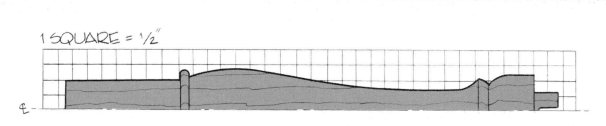

1 SQUARE = ½"

PEDESTAL PATTERN

You can rout the grooves with several different tools. The best is the overarm router, but it is not a common home workshop tool. A table-mounted router will do, but only if you use special 2"-long router bits. Standard bits aren't long enough. The tool for most home craftsmen to use is the drill press.

You can use the drill press safely for this operation if you follow three important precautions. First, adjust it to its highest speed. Second, make shallow cuts, removing 1/16"-1/8" with each pass. Third, fit the bit in a homemade *collet* before mounting it in the chuck. A drill chuck cannot adequately support the shank of the bit against side thrust, and the bit may bend or break. Make a collet by cutting a slot down the length of a bronze bushing. Insert a ¾" straight bit in this collet, then mount the collet in the chuck. (See Figure 1.)

To guide the workpiece, clamp a straightedge to the drill press worktable. To this, clamp a stop block to control the length of the cut. Align the post stock in the V-jig for cutting the first groove, and tighten the straps. Adjust the height of the bit for the first pass. Cut very slowly, keeping the V-jig pressed firmly against the straightedge.

When you finish the pass, lower the bit slightly and repeat. Continue until you have cut the groove ½" deep. (See Figure 2.) Realign the stock in the jig to cut the second and the third grooves.

TRY THIS! Feed the stock so the bit rotation forces the workpiece against the straightedge. Since the bit rotates clockwise, the straightedge should be to the left of the bit as you feed the stock away from you, onto the bit.

After you machine the grooves, square the stopped ends with a chisel. (See Figure 3.) Carefully test fit the legs in the grooves. If the legs are too tight, pare stock from the sides of the grooves with a chisel. *Hint:* It's better to have too tight a fit than too loose a fit. This is why you plane the leg stock slightly thicker than ¾", as mentioned in Step 1.

1/To rout safely with a drill press, make a router-bit collet from a ¼" I.D. bushing. Cut a slot in the bushing with a hacksaw.

2/Using your drill press as an overarm router, cut the grooves. Since the drill press turns much more slowly than a router, feed the stock very slowly and make very shallow cuts on each pass.

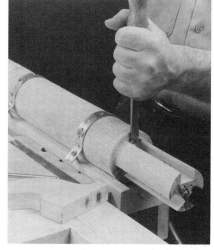

3/Square the ends of the grooves with a chisel. Use the V-jig to hold the stock while you work.

7

Finish turning the post. Mount the post on the lathe again, and complete the turning. (See Figure 4.) Turn the 1⅜″ tenon at the top of the post. Use the pivot block to gauge the precise diameter of this tenon. As you approach the correct diameter, remove the post from the lathe, and check the tenon's fit in the round mortise. If the fit is too tight, return the post to the lathe and remove a little more stock. Stop turning when the tenon fits the mortise easily, but without play.

Finish sand the completed post on the lathe, except for the upper and lower ends (the grooves and the tenon). Remove the post from the lathe and rest it in the V-jig — there's no need to strap it. Cut off *most* of the extra stock — leave the post about ¹⁄₁₆″ long on each end. On a band

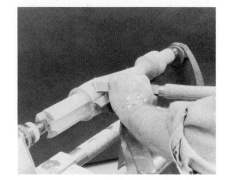

4/After cutting the grooves, replace the post on the lathe and finish turning it. Be careful not to turn the section with the grooves. If you do, the chisel may catch in one of them and ruin the post.

saw, cut the slot in the tenon for the wedge. The orientation of this slot is very important. It must be perpendicular to one of the grooves.

8

Assemble the legs, post, and pivot block. Glue the legs into the grooves. To clamp them, cut an old inner tube in 1″-wide strips. Tie three or four into one long strip, then wrap it around the post, over one leg and under the next, as shown in Figure 5. Stretch the strip tight as you wrap.

After the glue sets, remove the inner tube strip. Drill six ¼″-diameter, 1″-deep holes in the bottom of the post, as shown in the *Foot-to-Post Joinery Detail*. Each hole should straddle the joint between the leg and the post. Glue a ¼″-diameter dowel in each hole as a key. After the glue dries, trim the dowels and sand the bottom of the post flush with the legs.

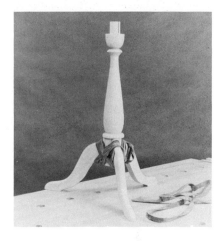

5/Use strips cut from an old inner tube to hold the legs to the post as you glue them together. Stretch them tight — the combined pressure will keep the legs tighter and more secure than any other clamping system you can devise.

TRY THIS! To sand the post's bottom, make a disk sander from a small lathe faceplate. Attach sandpaper to the faceplate with spray adhesive. Set the lathe on low speed and hold the assembly gently against the spinning disk.

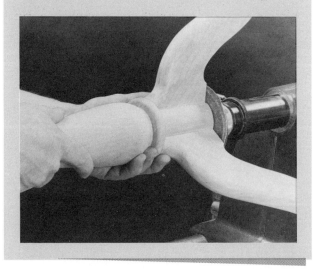

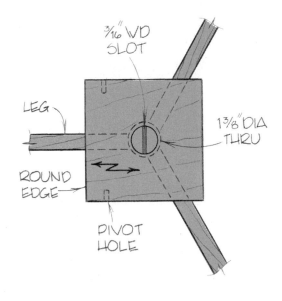

³⁄₁₆″ WD SLOT

LEG

1⅜″ DIA THRU

ROUND EDGE

PIVOT HOLE

**LEG-POST-PIVOT BLOCK
ALIGNMENT DETAIL**

Glue the pivot block to the top of the post, *rounded edge UP,* fitting it over the tenon. Cut a small wedge from scrap stock, and drive it into the tenon slot to tighten the tenon in the round mortise. After the glue dries, sand the wedge and the tenon flush with the top surface of the pivot block.

Note: The alignment of the pivot block, the wedge, and the legs is crucial. The correct alignment is shown in the *Leg-Post-Pivot Block Alignment Detail.* The grain of the pivot block must run perpendicular to the wedge. The edges of the block with the pivot holes must be parallel to one leg — the same leg that is held perpendicular to the wedge. This arrangement does two things: 1. It prevents the wedge from splitting the pivot block. 2. It allows you to store the candlestand as close to the wall as possible when the top is tipped up (and facing out).

9 **Attach the top.** Once again, turn the top upside down on your workbench. Then turn the leg-and-post assembly upside down on the top. Insert the metal pivots in the pivot block and the braces. Position each brace so that there is a $\frac{1}{16}''$ gap between it and the pivot block. Attach the braces to the top with round-head wood screws and washers. Do *not* glue the braces to the top.

Turn the candlestand upright, and check the tilting action of the top. It should tilt to 90° (vertical) and stop. If it rubs on the pivot block, remove the top by unscrewing the braces and sand stock from the block's rounded edge. Replace the top and check the action again.

When the top tilts properly, tip it to the vertical position. Trace the curve of the block on the inside of one of the braces. Remove that brace and drill a $\frac{1}{4}''$-diameter hole through it. The *edge* of this hole should just touch the line you made *above* the curve.

Replace the brace, and tilt the top to the horizontal position. Using the hole you just drilled as a guide, drill a $\frac{1}{4}''$-diameter, $\frac{3}{4}''$-deep hole into the pivot block. Insert a wooden pin with a $\frac{1}{4}''$ shank through the hole in the brace and into the block. This pin will keep the candlestand top from tipping up when it's supposed to be horizontal, and from falling back when it's supposed to be vertical.

Note: You can buy these pins from most woodworking supply centers. Or you can turn one on your lathe from $\frac{1}{2}''$ dowel stock. Refer to the *Locking Pin Detail* for the dimensions.

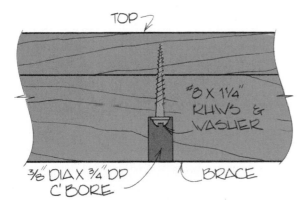

BRACE-TO-TOP JOINERY DETAIL

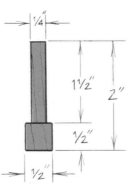

LOCKING PIN DETAIL

10 **Finish the completed candlestand.** Disassemble the top and the braces from the leg assembly, and remove the metal pivot pins. Do any touch-up sanding necessary, then apply a finish to the piece. Be sure to apply as many coats to the underside of the top as you do to the topside. This will keep it from warping. When the finish dries, rub it down with steel wool and paste wax. Then reassemble the candlestand.

Pewter Bench

Large shelving units are almost nonexistent in country furniture. Our ancestors didn't have the same need for shelves that we do. The typical library consisted of a single book (the Bible). Knickknacks were uncommon in country households. To be able to collect such things — to have the room to display them — was a true luxury. Consequently, if you search through country antiques collections for a large shelving unit for your living room or den, you'll have to look long and hard.

Country folks occasionally did create pieces of furniture for storing their dishes. Most were small wall-hung racks, but if there were a lot of family members — and the household collection of dinnerware was very large — then the piece might be a stand-alone floor unit. The floor units were called plate benches (or pewter benches, if the plates and cups were cast of that material). You'll find these benches hold books and collectibles just as well as dinnerware.

This contemporary pewter bench is adapted from an antique made by New England settlers in the early eighteenth century. The distinctive profile of the sides was a design characteristic of William and Mary furniture, which was in vogue at that time. Most of the shelves are set in tight-fitting dadoes to keep the piece rigid. Several of the lower shelves, however, rest on movable pegs so you can adjust the spacing of them.

Materials List

FINISHED DIMENSIONS

PARTS

A. Sides (2)   ¾″ x 9″ x 65½″
B. Top shelf   ¾″ x 4″ x 24¼″
C. Second shelf   ¾″ x 5″ x 24¼″
D. Third shelf   ¾″ x 6″ x 24¼″
E. Fourth shelf   ¾″ x 7″ x 24¼″
F. Fifth/bottom shelves (2)   ¾″ x 9″ x 24¼″
G. Adjustable shelves (3-4)   ¾″ x 9″ x 23⅜″
H. Apron   ¾″ x 3½″ x 23½″
J. Braces (2)   ¾″ x 3¼″ x 3¼″

HARDWARE

#10 x 1¼″ Flathead wood screws (28–36)
Pin-style shelving supports or ¼″-diameter dowels (12–16)

EXPLODED VIEW

1

Cut the parts to size.   Country craftsmen built benches and shelves like these from a variety of different woods — walnut, cherry, maple, and pine, to name a few. If the piece was to be painted, the woodworker usually selected "informal," inexpensive, easy-to-work stock such as white pine. The pewter bench shown was built of poplar.

To build the bench, you'll need approximately 22 board feet of 4/4 (four quarters) lumber. Plane this stock to ¾" thick, then cut all the parts to the sizes shown on the Materials List.

If you will paint the bench, and are using inexpensive wood, fill all knotholes and other defects.

2

Make the dadoes in the sides.   The fixed shelves are held to the sides by ¾"-wide, ⅜"-deep dadoes. You can make these joints with either a dado cutter or a router. A router probably is, perhaps, the easier tool to use, since you can do both sides simultaneously.

Lay the side boards edge to edge on your workbench and clamp them down. Enlarge the *Side Top Pattern* and trace it onto both boards. Carefully mark the locations of the dadoes, and be certain that they line up with the protrusions or "noses" on the pattern. Remember, the sides must be mirror images of each other. The pattern on one side piece should face left; on the other, it should face right.

Clamp a straightedge across the two workpieces to guide the router, and cut the dadoes with a ¾"-diameter straight bit. (See Figure 1.) Rout both boards at once, making several passes — each ⅛" deeper — to completely rout each set of dadoes. When you've finished one set, move the straightedge and make another. Continue until you have routed all the dadoes.

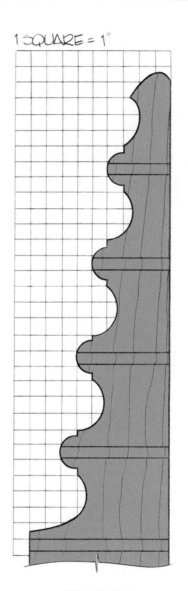

1 SQUARE = 1"

SIDE TOP PATTERN

1/Clamp the sides edge to edge on your workbench so that you can rout both boards at the same time. A homemade T-square jig simplifies this operation. The leg of the "T" guides the router, and the cross helps to accurately position the jig.

3 ***Drill the support pin holes in the sides.***
While the sides are still clamped edge to edge on
your workbench, lay out the positions of the holes for
the pins that support the adjustable shelves, as shown in
the *Side Layout*. Drill these ¼″-diameter holes ⅜″ deep.

TRY THIS! To simplify drilling two dozen
precisely positioned holes in each side, clamp a
fence or a straightedge to the worktable of your
drill press to guide the workpiece. Properly positioned, the fence will ensure that the holes are 2″
from the edge, and you can concentrate on getting
the proper spacing between holes. If you drill the
holes with a hand-held drill, clamp a fence to the
workpiece.

4 ***Cut the contoured parts.*** Enlarge the *Side
Bottom Pattern* and the *Apron Pattern,* and trace
them onto the stock. Cut out all the contoured parts —
including the sides — with a band saw or saber saw. Sand
the sawed edges to remove the saw marks.

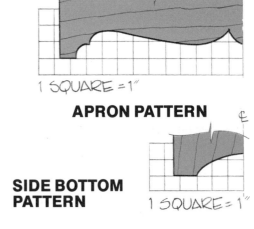

1 SQUARE = 1″

APRON PATTERN

**SIDE BOTTOM
PATTERN**

1 SQUARE = 1″

5 ***Assemble the project.*** Finish sand all the
parts. Glue the fixed shelves in their dadoes, then
reinforce the joints with screws. Glue the aprons and
the brackets in place, and again reinforce with screws.

Counterbore and countersink all the screws, and cover
the heads with wooden plugs. This will make the pewter
bench look as if it were pegged together.

TRY THIS! To give the pewter bench an old-
time look, use cut nails instead of screws. These
nails have square shanks and almost no head. Drill
pilot holes (to keep them from splitting the stock),
then drive the nails. Leave the heads flush with the
surface, and don't cover them.

6 ***Finish the completed pewter bench.***
Do any touch-up sanding necessary, and apply
a finish. If you use a finish that builds up on the surface
of the wood, such as varnish or paint, it will collect in
the support pin holes, making it hard for you to insert
the pins. Don't fret. Let the finish dry, then clean out the
holes with a ¼″-diameter twist bit and an electric drill.
Finally, insert the pins and lay the shelves in place.

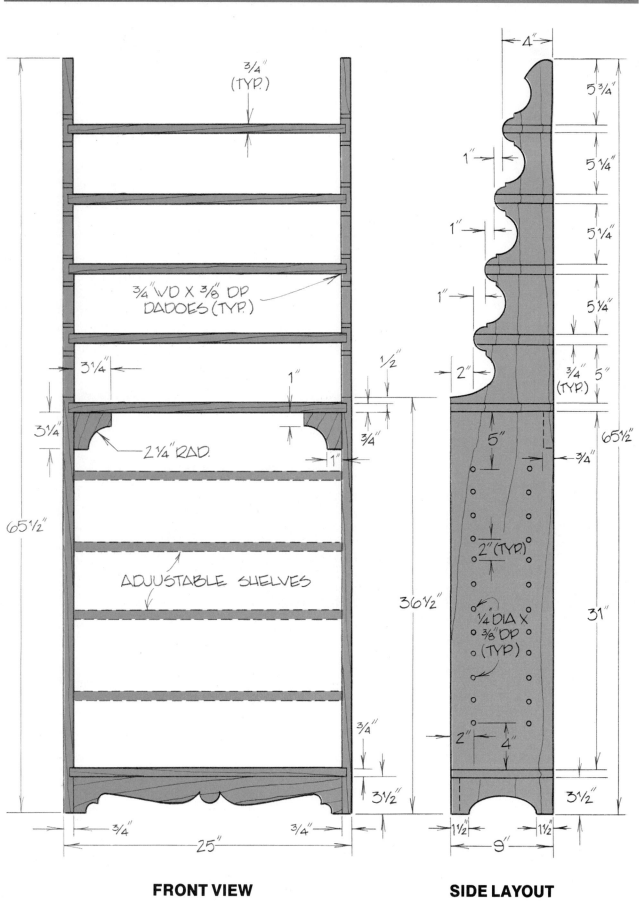

3/4"
(TYP.)

3/4" WD X 3/8" DP
DADOES (TYP.)

3 1/4"

1"

1/2"

3 1/4"

2 1/4" RAD.

3/4"

1"

ADJUSTABLE SHELVES

65 1/2"

36 1/2"

3/4"

3/4"

3 1/2"

3/4"

25"

4"

5 3/4"

1"

5 1/4"

1"

5 1/4"

1"

5 1/4"

2"

3/4"
(TYP.)

5"

5"

65 1/2"

3/4"

2" (TYP.)

1/4" DIA X
3/8" DP
(TYP.)

31"

2"

4"

3 1/2"

1 1/2"

1 1/2"

9"

FRONT VIEW　　　　**SIDE LAYOUT**

Uncle Sam Whirligig

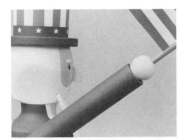

No other form of folk art is quite so typically American as the whirligig.

This wind toy evolved long before the discovery of the New World. But nowhere was it quite so popular as in America. From its beginnings, America was a nation of tinkerers, and these miniature wind-driven machines captured the American imagination. Just as the intricate lines of a Philadelphia highboy and the austere grace of a Shaker chair expressed the poetry in an American craftsman's soul, or the steam locomotive and the airplane reflected his dreams, the whirligig echoed his humor.

Many American whirligigs expressed patriotism. Caricatures of Lady Liberty and Uncle Sam were popular whirligigs, particularly around the 1876 Centennial celebration. This Uncle Sam waves two 37-star flags every time the wind picks up. (Remember, there were just 37 states in the Union in 1876.)

Although Uncle Sam looks carved, he's not. The body is turned on a lathe, then compound-cut on a band saw to create the shape of the head and the torso. The other parts are either cut to shape or made from dowels and beads, then joined to the body. Soften the hard edges with sandpaper and presto! You have a realistic figure in a top hat. ✸

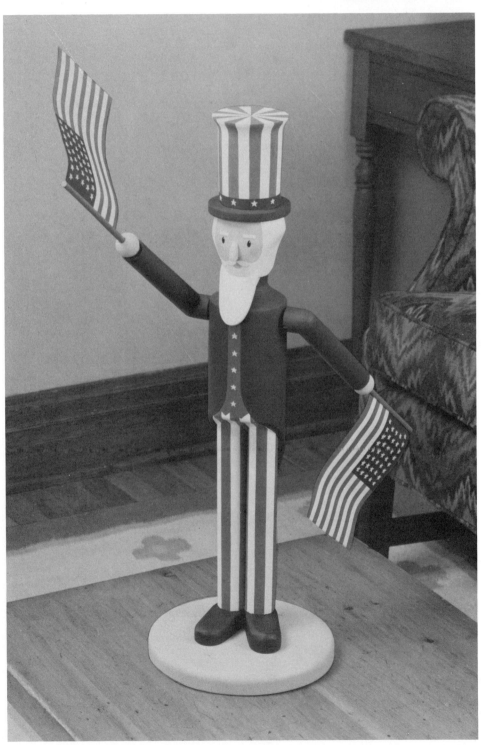

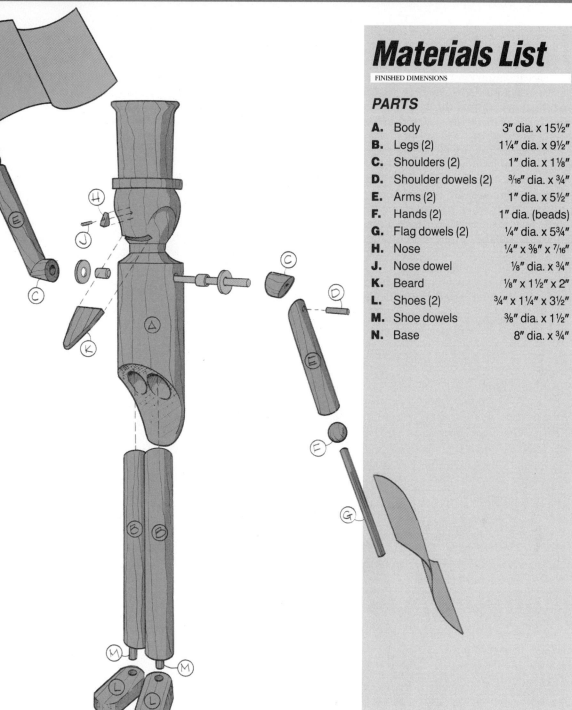

EXPLODED VIEW

Materials List

FINISHED DIMENSIONS

PARTS

A.	Body	3″ dia. x 15½″
B.	Legs (2)	1¼″ dia. x 9½″
C.	Shoulders (2)	1″ dia. x 1⅛″
D.	Shoulder dowels (2)	3/16″ dia. x ¾″
E.	Arms (2)	1″ dia. x 5½″
F.	Hands (2)	1″ dia. (beads)
G.	Flag dowels (2)	¼″ dia. x 5¾″
H.	Nose	¼″ x ⅜″ x 7/16″
J.	Nose dowel	⅛″ dia. x ¾″
K.	Beard	⅛″ x 1½″ x 2″
L.	Shoes (2)	¾″ x 1¼″ x 3½″
M.	Shoe dowels	⅜″ dia. x 1½″
N.	Base	8″ dia. x ¾″

HARDWARE

4″ x 6″ Aluminum flashing (2 pieces)
3/16″ dia. x 4 3/16″ Metal rod
¼″ I.D. x ½″ Copper tubing (2 pieces)
#10 Flat washers (2)
#10 x 1½″ Flathead wood screws (2)

1 Select the materials.

Select the materials. While this project is a great country accent for your living room, you can also use it outdoors where it will catch the breeze. Where you will display the whirligig has a bearing on your choice of materials — wood, hardware, and glue.

For a whirligig that will be out in the weather, select a wood that weathers well but is strong enough to stand up to constant motion. The traditional choices for outdoor projects — cedar, redwood, and cypress — are too soft and break easily. Pressure-treated wood often warps and splits when you cut it into small pieces. Early American craftsmen made their whirligigs from eastern white pine, but their stock was cut from virgin timber. The annual rings were close together and evenly spaced, and this helped keep the wood from distorting or decaying. Today's white pine is cut from fast-growing trees, and it doesn't stand up to the weather as well.

Poplar is a good choice. It will weather well if it's coated with a water seal before you paint it. The best choice is a tropical wood — mahogany. It's weather-resistant, strong, and is easily worked. It's expensive, but you need so little wood that the overall cost will be low.

For the metal parts, choose a material that won't rust. Not only will rusting nails and screws stain the project, they'll come loose as they corrode away. Use hardware made from galvanized or stainless steel, brass, or bronze.

Use a waterproof glue such as resorcinol or epoxy. When gluing metal to wood — for instance, when attaching the arms to the axle — a product called PC-7, made by the Protective Coating Company of Allentown, Pennsylvania, works best. This epoxy putty is especially formulated to bond dissimilar surfaces. It can also be used as a wood filler to mend mistakes.

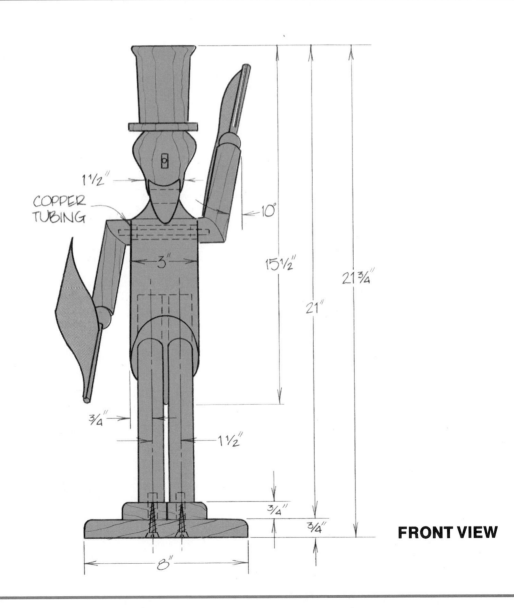

FRONT VIEW

2

Turn the dowels and beads. If you're making this project for display indoors, use ordinary wooden beads, dowels, and closet pole to make the hands, arms, and legs. But if it is for the outdoors, you must turn these parts — you can't purchase poplar or mahogany dowels.

3

Cut the parts to size. Cut the wooden parts — with the exception of the body — to the sizes shown in the Materials List. Cut the body at least 1″ longer than the specified length, so that you have some extra stock to mount it on the lathe. Miter one end of each arm and shoulder at 50°.

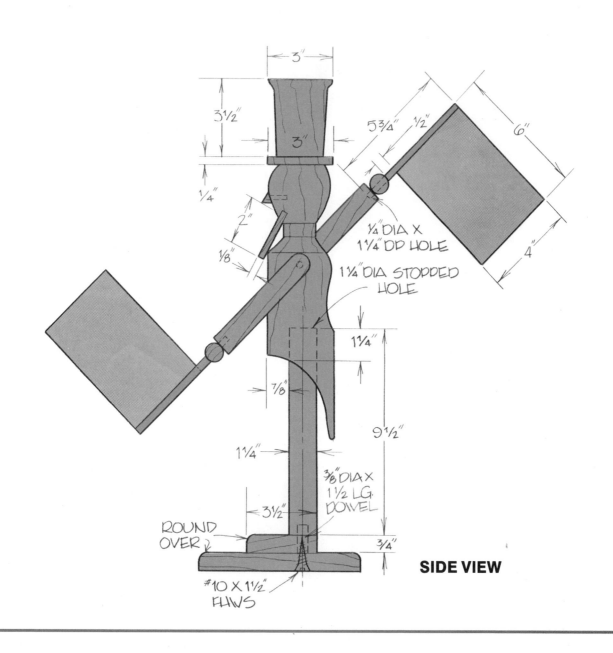

SIDE VIEW

4 *Turn the body.* Enlarge the *Body Turning and Cutting Pattern* and trace it on stiff poster board. With scissors, cut *two* templates — a negative (or outline) of the *turned* profile, and a positive (or silhouette) of the *sawed* profile. Using the sawing template, mark the location of the 5/16″-diameter axle hole on the body stock. Drill the hole.

Mount the stock on your lathe and turn a straight 3″-diameter cylinder. From this cylinder, create the shape of the body. (See Figure 1.) Use the turning template to gauge your progress as you work. Be careful to keep the torso, hat brim, and top of the hat a uniform diameter, so that in the next step the body will rest securely in the V-jig. Finish sand the turning on the lathe.

1/To make the body, first turn the stock on the lathe. Use a template to gauge the contours as you work. Keep the torso, hat brim, and top of the hat at the same diameter so that the stock will rest securely in the V-jig.

FIRST SET OF CUTS

1/8″ WD X 1/2″ DP SLOT FOR BEARD

5/16″ DIA HOLE THRU

SECOND SET OF CUTS

BODY TURNING AND CUTTING PATTERN

1 SQUARE = 1/2″

5 *Cut the shape of the body.* From a scrap of 2 x 4, make a V-jig as shown in the *V-Jig Detail*. Do *not* use a good V-jig that you may already have made — you're going to saw up this jig in the process of shaping the body.

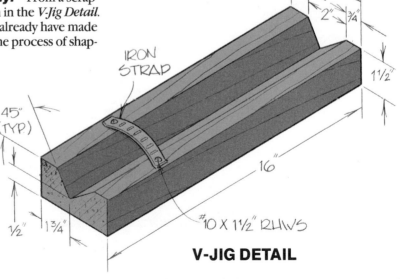

3 1/2″
3/4
2″ 3/4
1 1/2″

IRON STRAP

45° (TYP.)

16″

1/2″ 1 3/4″

#10 X 1 1/2″ RHWS

V-JIG DETAIL

Mount the turning in the jig, and tighten the strap. Using the sawing template, trace the first set of cuts on the stock. Because the template is flat and the stock is round, you won't be able to mark the cuts precisely. Don't worry — these cuts aren't critical. Slight variations will only make your Uncle Sam distinct from the one shown.

With a band saw, cut the hollows for the cheeks. (See Figure 2.) Loosen the strap, turn the body 90°, and tighten the strap again. Mark, then make the second set of cuts — the slot for the beard, the hollow of the back, and the coattails.

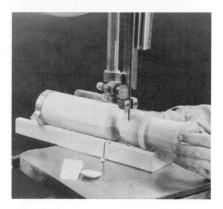

2/Strap the body turning in a V-jig and cut the final profile with a band saw. You'll cut up the V-jig as you saw the body, so be careful to position the metal strap where you won't hit it with the saw blade.

6 **Bore the holes for the legs.** With the turning still strapped in the jig, bore the holes for the legs. Carefully position the body and jig on the worktable of your drill press, then clamp them securely in place. Drill the leg holes, as shown in the *Front View* and the *Side View.* Bore each hole very slowly, feeding the bit with a very light pressure, to keep the body from shifting. (See Figure 3.)

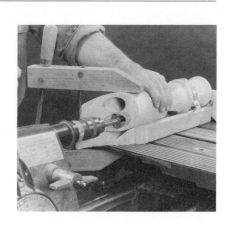

3/Use the V-jig to hold the body while you bore the holes for the legs. Multispur and Forstner bits work best for this step. Either will cut end grain cleanly and leave a flat-bottomed hole.

7 **Cut the shapes of the beard, nose, feet, and base.** Trace the *Beard Pattern* and *Nose Pattern* onto the appropriate stock. Lay out the shapes of the feet and the base. Cut each of these pieces on a band saw. Sand the sawed edges, and round over the top edge of the base and the toes of the feet.

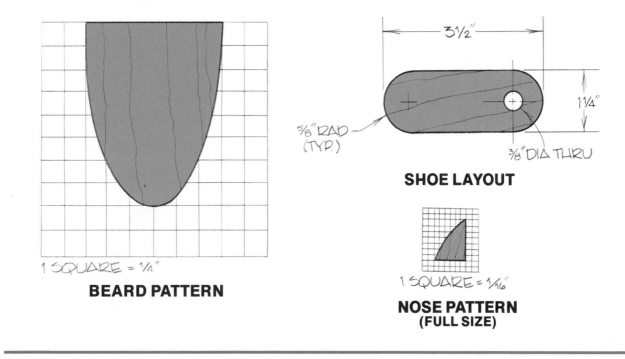

1 SQUARE = ¼"

BEARD PATTERN

3½"

5/8" RAD (TYP.)

1¼"

3/8" DIA THRU

SHOE LAYOUT

1 SQUARE = ⅟₁₆"

NOSE PATTERN
(FULL SIZE)

8

Assemble the arms. Glue the shoulders and the hands to the arms, and let the glue dry completely (overnight). Carefully bore 3/16″-diameter holes completely through the shoulders and the arms, as shown in the *Arm Layout*. Glue 3/4″ lengths of 3/16″-diameter dowel in these holes to reinforce the glue joints. Drive the dowels in from the shoulder side, so that they only partially plug the holes.

Bore 1/4″-diameter, 1 1/4″-deep holes through the hands and into the arms. These holes will hold flags.

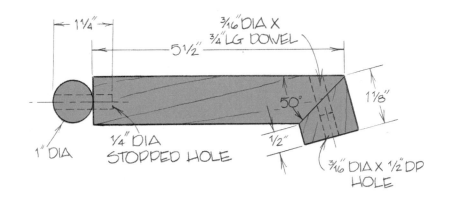

ARM LAYOUT

9

Make the flags. With tin snips, cut two 4″ x 6″ rectangles from a sheet of aluminum flashing. On your band saw, saw a 4″-long slot down the center of the flag dowels. Using an epoxy putty, glue the aluminum rectangles in the slots. Let the epoxy dry overnight, then bend the aluminum so that each flag has a slight wave.

10

Assemble the whirligig. Drive two 1/2″ lengths of 1/4″ I.D. copper tubing into the axle hole — one in either end of the hole. These will serve as bushings for the axle.

Using a rasp and a file, blend the turned and the sawed contours. Finish sand all the wooden parts. Glue the feet to the legs and the nose to the face. After the glue sets, drill holes, and drive dowels into them to reinforce the glue joints.

Glue the beard in its slot and the legs in their holes. Splay the feet slightly, as shown in the *Top View.* Then mount the base on the body assembly with wood screws. (Don't glue the base to the feet — it will be removed to make it easier to paint the whirligig.)

Insert the axle through the body and put flat washers over the ends. Temporarily fit the arm assemblies on the axle to check its length. The arms must not pinch the washers against the body; a small amount of play is necessary, just about 1/16″. If the axle is too long, cut or file a little metal from the end. If it's too short, you'll have to cut a new axle.

When you're certain the axle is the proper length, remove the arms and the axle from the body. Slightly flatten the ends of the axle with a hammer. (See Figure 4.)

Reassemble the parts, using epoxy putty to glue the wooden arms to the metal axle. Carefully position the arms so that one will point straight up when the other is straight down. Let the epoxy harden overnight.

4/Flatten the ends of the axle before you glue the arms to it. This will give the epoxy a rough surface to adhere to, and help keep the axle tight in the arms.

TRY THIS! An air-filled sanding drum is the ideal drill press or lathe accessory to use to blend the body's turned and sawed contours. The drum inflates with a bicycle pump or air compressor.

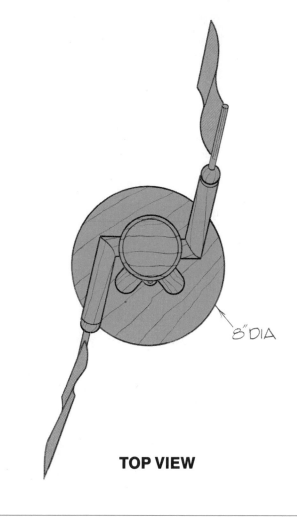

8" DIA

TOP VIEW

11 Paint the whirligig.

Remove Uncle Sam from his base, and touch him up with fine sandpaper. Spray the aluminum flags with zinc chromate primer so that paint will adhere to them, and let the primer dry thoroughly.

Lightly pencil the stars and the stripes onto both the Uncle Sam and his flags. Paint his suit, hat, and flags a patriotic red, white, and blue. Color his beard white, and his face and hands flesh tones. Paint the flag dowels and the shoes a dark brown or black — you may even want to give him some white spats. Finally, make the base a neutral color, such as a light gray blue.

You can use a variety of paints to color this project. Perhaps the easiest to use — for both indoor *and* outdoor whirligigs — are artist's colors (which come in tubes). Both oils and acrylics stand up well in the weather, and they can be blended to create an infinite variety of shades. The only problem is that once you've mixed a color, you may not be able to match it exactly. The first batch you mix of each color has to be large enough to complete the job.

Note: Some hobby stores offer a large selection of ready-mixed acrylic colors in 1-2 oz. bottles.

12 Position the flags.

When the paint dries, put Uncle Sam back on his base. Glue the flags in his hands, turning them slightly so that one flag angles in and the other angles out, as you look at the whirligig

from the top. Then set the completed whirligig near an open window, a fan, or a spot in your garden where it will catch a breeze.

Rocking Chair

The rocking chair or "rocker" is a purely American invention. The design first appeared in New England during the eighteenth century, and rockers quickly became popular. Before the century was out, craftsmen throughout the states were making several styles, both plain and fancy.

Perhaps the best-known makers of plain, country-style rocking chairs were a religious group called the United Society of Believers in Christ's Second Reappearing — better known as the Shakers. Shaker craftsmen fervently believed their handiwork was a form of worship. Because of the care they took in making it, their furniture was highly prized. Their chairs and rockers in particular enjoyed a reputation for good design, durable materials, and excellent craftsmanship.

This rocking chair was built in the tradition of the Union Village Shakers.

Union Village, near Lebanon, Ohio, was one of the westernmost communities, and the designs of its craftsmen tended to be simpler and more primitive — more country, perhaps — than those of its eastern counterparts. Most of the frame parts are turned cylinders, joined by round mortises and tenons. The only decorations are the pommels topping the back posts and the fretwork at the front of the rockers. The seat and the back of the chair are woven from narrow cloth tape or "listing" in a herringbone pattern. ✹

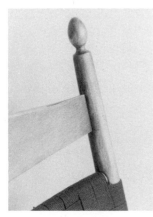

Materials List

FINISHED DIMENSIONS

PARTS

A. Back posts (2)   1⅜″ dia. x 38¼″

B. Front legs (2)   1⅜″ dia. x 17″

C. Back seat stretcher   1″ dia. x 15⅛″

D. Side seat stretchers (2)   1″ dia. x 16⅛″

E. Front seat stretcher   1″ dia. x 19⅜″

F. Back rung   ¾″ dia. x 15⅛″

G. Side rungs (4)   ¾″ dia. x 16⅛″

H. Front rungs (2)   ¾″ dia. x 19⅜″

J. Lower back stretcher   ¾″ x 15⅝″

K. Upper back stretcher   ¾″ dia. x 16⅜″

L. Backrest   ¼″ x 2¾″ x 16⅜″

M. Rockers (2)   ⅜″ x 4¼″ x 28½″

N. Dowels (2)   ¼″ dia. x ⅝″

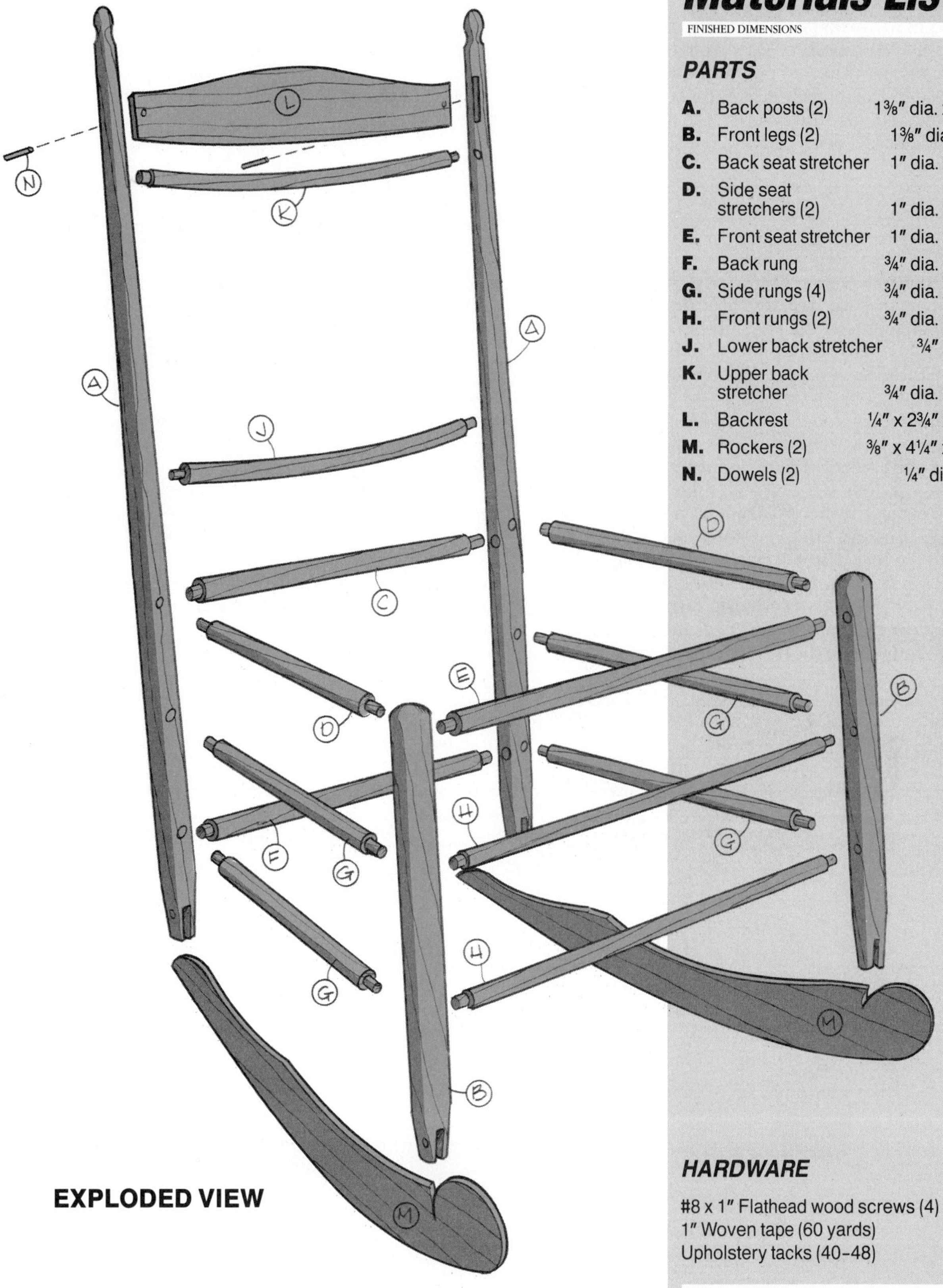

EXPLODED VIEW

HARDWARE

#8 x 1″ Flathead wood screws (4)
1″ Woven tape (60 yards)
Upholstery tacks (40–48)

1

Cut all parts to rough size. Select clear, straight hardwood stock for this project. Stock with knots, burls and other defects may split on the lathe or — what could be worse? — give way when someone sits on the rocker. Traditionally, Shaker rockers were made from maple or birch. However, you can use cherry, walnut, oak, or hickory.

Cut the turning blanks slightly larger than what is specified in the Materials List. For turning, you want the stock to be 1/4"-1/2" wider and thicker, and 2"-3" longer than the finished dimensions. Cut the backrest and the back stretchers 4"-6" longer than needed. You'll need this extra length when you bend these parts.

2

Turn the legs, rungs, and stretchers. Since the parts have very little decoration, the turning is straightforward. The only beads and coves you have to turn are on the pommels. These aren't critical to the design; you may change them or even eliminate them.

The round tenons on the ends of the rungs and stretchers are, however, critical. These tenons (and their shoulders) give strength and stability to the frame. Turn the tenons carefully, working with a shopmade tenon gauge. To make it, drill a 3/4"-diameter hole in a piece of scrap wood, and cut a slot from the outside edge of the scrap into the hole. Carefully rasp away the edges of the slot until it is *precisely* 5/8" wide — as wide as the diameter of the tenons you want to turn. Turn each tenon until it is *slightly* larger than 5/8" in diameter. Set aside the chisel and take up the tenon gauge and sandpaper.

1/Use sandpaper to remove the last little bit of stock from the tenon. It removes stock more slowly than a chisel, and there's less chance that you will accidentally remove too much. Using a shopmade tenon gauge will help you know when the tenon is at the right diameter.

Hold the gauge against the tenon from one side, while you sand it from the other. (See Figure 1.) When the gauge slips over the tenon, stop sanding *immediately* — the tenon is properly sized.

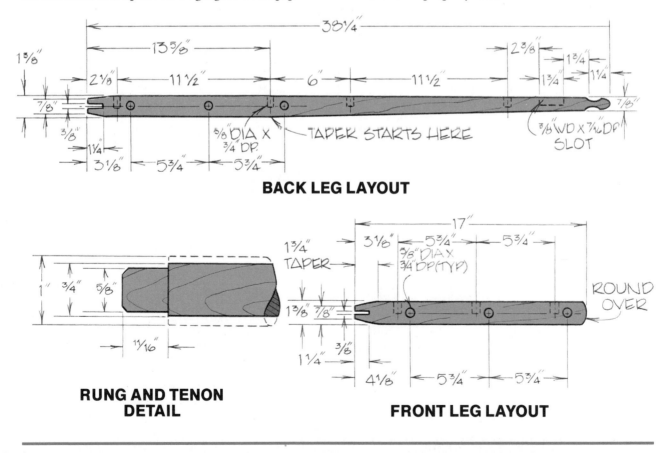

BACK LEG LAYOUT

RUNG AND TENON DETAIL

FRONT LEG LAYOUT

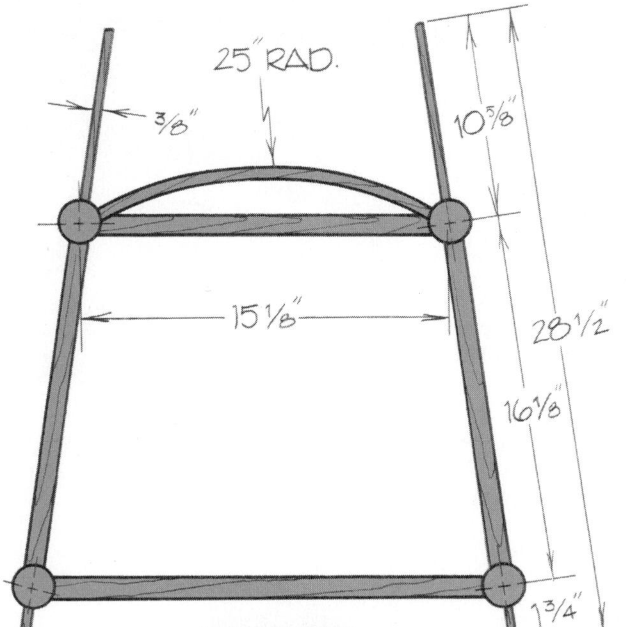
25" RAD.
3/8"
10 5/8"
15 1/8"
28 1/2"
16 1/8"
1 3/4"

TOP VIEW
(WITHOUT SEAT)

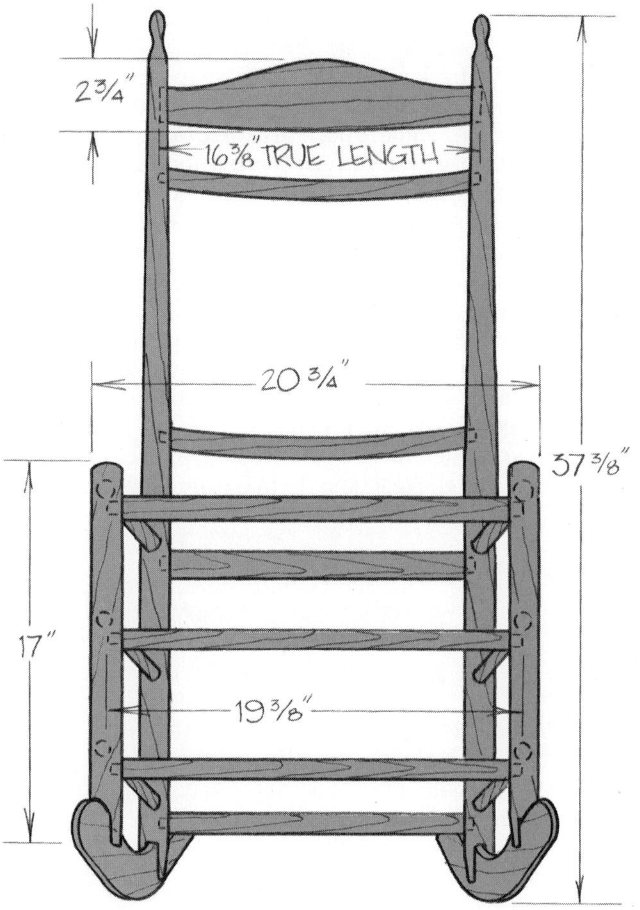
2 3/4"
16 3/8" TRUE LENGTH
20 3/4"
37 3/8"
17"
19 3/8"

FRONT VIEW
(WITHOUT SEAT)

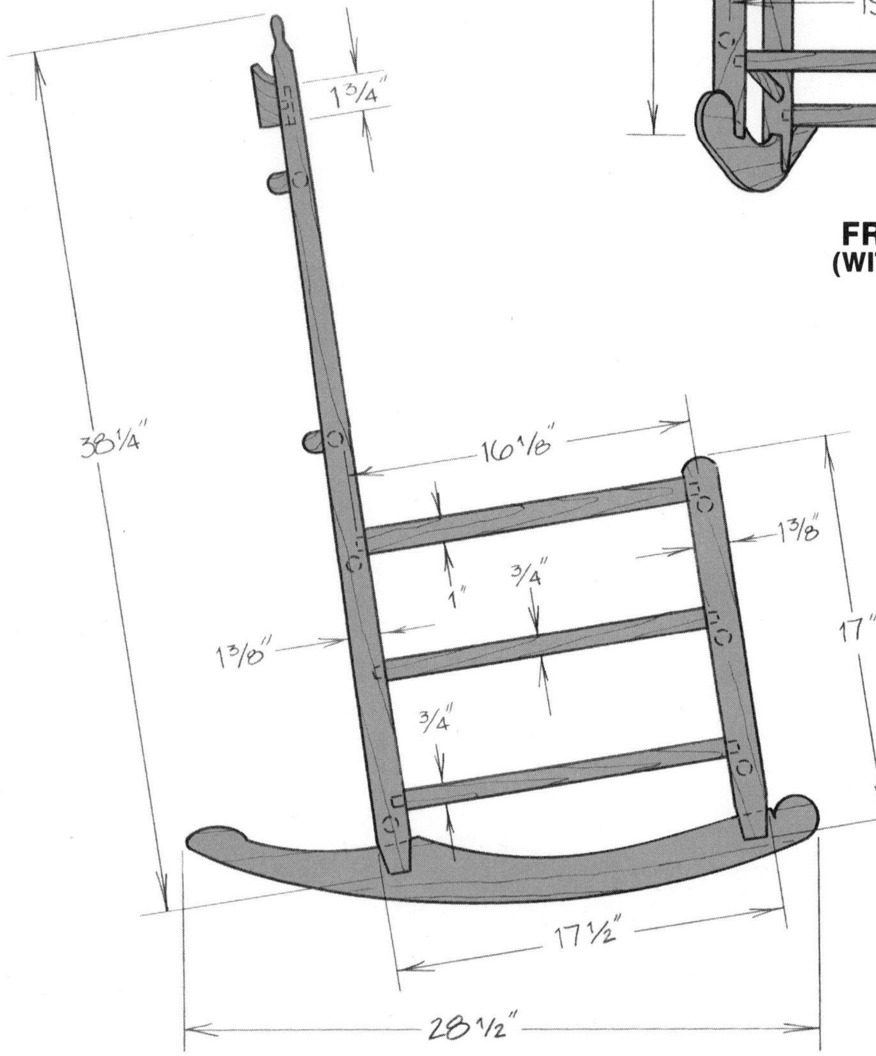
1 3/4"
38 1/4"
16 1/8"
1 3/8"
1"
3/4"
17"
1 3/8"
3/4"
17 1/2"
28 1/2"

SIDE VIEW
(WITHOUT SEAT)

To turn the back posts, you may have to modify your lathe slightly. Most home workshop lathes have a capacity of about 36″, and the posts are 38¼″ long. If you're determined, however, you can work around this limitation. The tailstock and the tail center detach from most lathes. Build a separate mount for the tailstock/center and clamp it to your workbench or some other *sturdy* platform you can station near the lathe. (See Figure 2.) As long as you clamp the stock between the centers and work at low speeds, you can safely make a spindle turning several inches longer than the advertised capacity of your machine. To turn the full length of the stock, switch it end for end between the centers.

Finish sand each turned part on the lathe before you remove it from the machine. To make the surface as

2/With a little ingenuity, you can safely extend the capacity of a lathe (in this instance, a Shopsmith) to turn the back posts. You can also replace the bed tubes on many lathes with ordinary plumbing pipe. Some manufacturers offer bed extenders as accessories.

smooth as possible, sand with the lathe running down to 150# sandpaper. Then turn off the motor and give each piece a final hand sanding *with* the grain.

TRY THIS! All of the rocker's parts are fairly slender — the largest finished diameter is just 1⅜″. Because of this, you need to ensure that the spindles don't "whip" or bow on the lathe. Use just enough pressure between the centers to keep the stock firmly mounted in the lathe. When turning the longer pieces, use a steadyrest to keep them from whipping. Some manufacturers offer these as accessories, or you can make your own.

3 Shape the backrest and the rockers.

Enlarge the backrest pattern and the rocker pattern. Trace these onto the stock. Then cut out the shapes with a band saw or scroll saw. Smooth the sawed edges with a sander or a file.

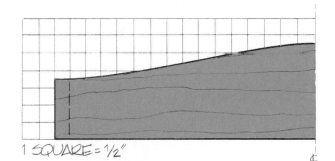

1 SQUARE = ½″

BACKREST PATTERN

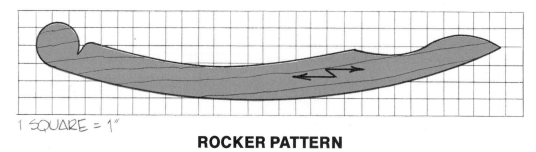

1 SQUARE = 1″

ROCKER PATTERN

4 Bend the backrest and the back stretchers.

The backrest and back stretchers must bow slightly to fit your back. Because the parts are thin, you can do this bending easily in a home workshop, without a steamer.

First, make a bending jig. This is nothing more than a block of wood, 3″ x 8″ x 16″, cut into two pieces. The cut is curved, and the curve is more pronounced than the one you want to achieve. After being bent in the jig, the parts will spring back slightly, so the radius of the

bending jig should be 20 percent smaller than the radius of the finished backrest. Since the radius you want to achieve is 25″, cut the bending jig at a 20″ radius.

Boil the backrest in a roasting pan for 45-60 minutes. Then place it in the jig, clamping the two halves together and bending the backrest. (See Figure 3.) Let it dry in the jig for at least two weeks, then repeat the process to bend the back stretchers. If you're in a hurry, you may want to make two jigs — one for the backrest and the other for the stretchers.

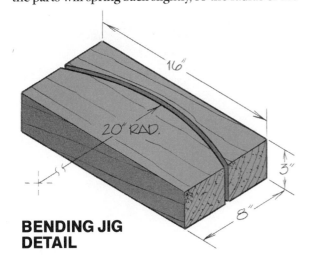

BENDING JIG DETAIL

3/To bend the back parts, boil them in water to make them flexible, then clamp them in a jig before they cool. As they cool, they will regain their rigidity and will assume the shape of the jig. To avoid pressing flat spots on the round back stretchers, make the jig out of a wood that is softer than they are. Or: Cut round-bottomed grooves in the adjoining halves of the jig with a gouge.

5 Drill the mortises in the legs and posts.

The mortises in each post and leg must line up properly with their counterparts in the other posts. There are two planes or "lines" of round mortises as you sight down the front legs — one for front rungs/stretchers and the other for the side rungs/stretchers/rockers. The back posts have three lines of mortises — side rungs/stretchers/rockers, back rung/seat stretcher, and the backrest/back stretcher. The *Mortise Layout* shows the orientation of one line to another. Mark the angles on the ends of the leg, then transfer them down the length of the stock using a long, V-shaped jig. Rest the stock in the jig and use one side of the "V" as a straightedge as you draw your lines. (See Figure 4.)

This V-jig also comes in handy when it's time to drill and rout the mortises. Secure the leg in the jig with metal straps and wood screws. (See Figure 5.) Clamp a fence to the drill press table to accurately position the stock under the bit, then drill all the round mortises. Cut the backrest mortises with an overarm router. For this operation, clamp a fence to the router table to guide the jig holding the workpiece.

Using a band saw, cut the slot mortises for the rockers. These mortises should be aligned with those for the side rungs and side stretchers.

4/To help you mark the position of the mortises, make a V-jig out of 1 x 2 stock and use it as a straightedge. Be sure to joint the edges of the 1 x 2's so that the straightedge is really straight.

5/You can use the V-jig to hold the legs and posts when you make the mortises. Use scraps of leather or rubber to keep the metal straps from marring the wood.

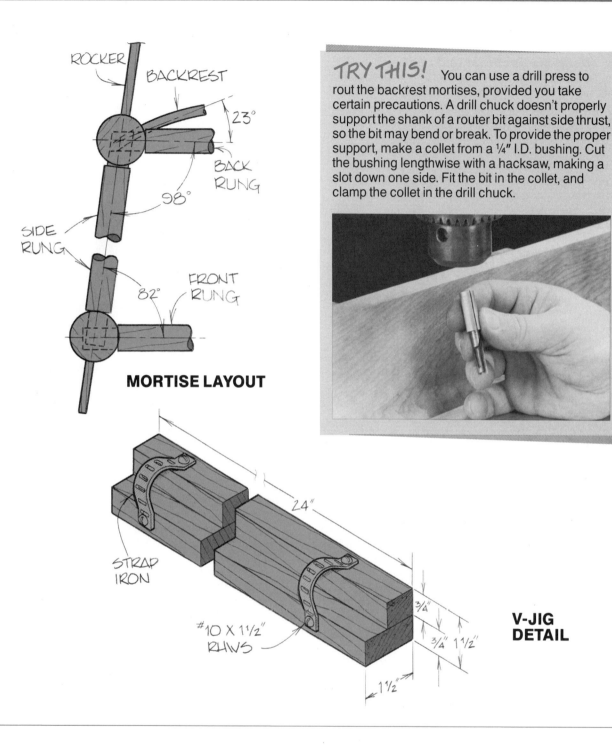

ROCKER
BACKREST
23°
BACK
RUNG
98°
SIDE
RUNG
82°
FRONT
RUNG

MORTISE LAYOUT

TRY THIS! You can use a drill press to rout the backrest mortises, provided you take certain precautions. A drill chuck doesn't properly support the shank of a router bit against side thrust, so the bit may bend or break. To provide the proper support, make a collet from a ¼″ I.D. bushing. Cut the bushing lengthwise with a hacksaw, making a slot down one side. Fit the bit in the collet, and clamp the collet in the drill chuck.

STRAP
IRON

24″

#10 X 1½″
RHWS

¾″
¾″ 1½″

1½″

**V-JIG
DETAIL**

6 **Assemble the frame.** Finish sand any parts that may still need it, then dry assemble the rocker frame. If everything fits properly, glue together the legs, rungs, stretchers, and backrest. (Don't attach the rockers yet.)

Glue won't hold the frame together forever. The frame flexes every time you sit on the rocker, and many of the glue joints eventually will pop. Traditionally, rockers are held together by tightly-woven seats and a few well-placed pegs. Peg the top backrest in the back posts. Drill stopped peg holes from the back.

Attach the rockers to the frame with flathead wood screws. Drive these screws through the bottom of the legs and posts and into the rockers from the *outside*. Do *not* glue the rockers in place. The screws make it easy to replace a rocker, should one break.

7

Apply a finish to the rocker. You'll want to finish your rocker *before* you weave the seat; it's too hard to do afterwards. Shaker craftsmen used a variety of finishes and stains, the most common being oil finish and milk paint.

8

Weave a seat and a back. The Shakers wove seats and backs of rush, splint, straw, cane, leather, even twisted paper. The seat they are best remembered for — the one that is the easiest to weave — is cloth tape. You can purchase the necessary tape from:

Shaker Workshops
P.O. Box 1028
Concord, MA 01742

Connecticut Cane and
Reed Company
P.O. Box 1276
Manchester, CT 06040

Begin weaving with the *warp* (front-to-back tape). Tack the lead end of a coil of tape to the back stretcher near the back leg. (See Figure 6.) Bring the coil over the back stretcher to the front stretcher, over and under it, then back under and over the back. Keep the tape stretched as tight as possible. Repeat the process until the back stretcher is covered. (See Figure 7.) When wrapping the last warp row, lap the tape over itself and tack it to the back stretcher. Since the front stretcher is slightly longer than the back stretcher, it won't be covered completely by the warp — yet. Leave an equal amount of front stretcher showing on either side, creating two triangular open spaces.

Stuff a foam rubber pad into the space between the top and bottom warps, then weave the *woof* (side-to-side tape). Tack the end of another coil to the side stretcher, near the back leg. Wrap the tape over the stretchers in the same manner as before, but weave the woof into the warp. (See Figure 8.) Weave over one and under one to make a checkerboard pattern. Weave over two and under two, skipping one at the beginning of each row, to create the herringbone pattern shown. Weave the same pattern on both the top and the bottom of the seat. If you have to splice two coils of tape, sew them together on the *underside* of the seat, where the splice won't show.

Fill in the triangular areas by weaving short lengths of warp tape into the woof. Pull the woof aside, and tack these warp tapes to the side stretchers. (See Figure 9.) Slide the woofs back in place to cover the tacks.

Weave the back in the same manner. However, since the back is almost square, you won't have to fill in odd-shaped areas with short lengths of tape.

For further information on this technique, consult "Chair Seat Weaving" by Marion Burr Sober, available from the Connecticut Cane and Reed Company.

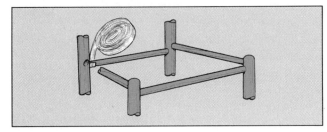

6/Tack the cloth tape to the back seat stretcher, near the back leg.

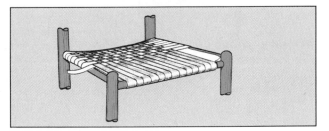

8/Insert foam padding between the top and bottom warps, then weave the woof tape.

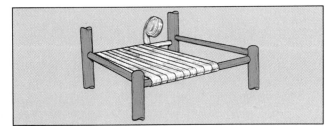

7/Wind the warp tape from back to front to back. Continue until you have *covered the entire seat, except for two triangular areas on either side.*

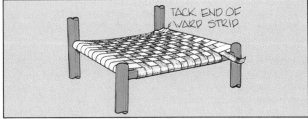

9/Finish by filling in the triangular areas with short lengths of warp tape. Pull the *woof aside and tack the ends to the side stretchers.*

Sailmaker's Bench

M any old-time craftsmen preferred to sit down on the job. Coopers, cobblers, tinkers, shingle-makers, basketweavers, and dozens of other tradespeople traditionally sat on low, broad benches that served as both seats and work surfaces. This is the origin of the term "work-bench." Sitting on a low workbench was an efficient (and restful) way to work. The few hand tools that an artisan needed could be arranged within easy reach on the bench.

Today's power tools are too large and too numerous for a craftsman to remain seated on a bench for very long. Most craft work is done standing at a power tool, and the legs of most workbenches have grown so that an artisan can work standing up. The low, broad benches of old have found other employment as coffee tables and television stands.

The sailmaker's bench is a typical example of these old country workbenches. It's a thick, strong slab of wood supported by heavy legs. Underneath the slab, there is a single drawer which, in the sailmaker's day, held needles, scissors, cords, and other tools and materials. The drawer rides on L-shaped brackets and can be opened from either side of the bench, making its contents more accessible.

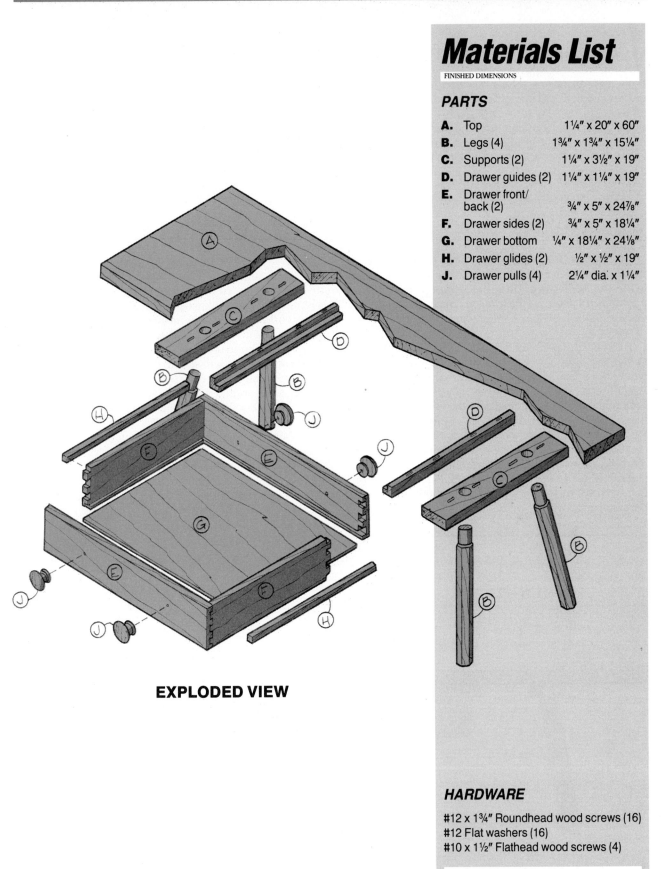

EXPLODED VIEW

Materials List

FINISHED DIMENSIONS

PARTS

A.	Top	1¼″ x 20″ x 60″
B.	Legs (4)	1¾″ x 1¾″ x 15¼″
C.	Supports (2)	1¼″ x 3½″ x 19″
D.	Drawer guides (2)	1¼″ x 1¼″ x 19″
E.	Drawer front/ back (2)	¾″ x 5″ x 24⅞″
F.	Drawer sides (2)	¾″ x 5″ x 18¼″
G.	Drawer bottom	¼″ x 18¼″ x 24⅛″
H.	Drawer glides (2)	½″ x ½″ x 19″
J.	Drawer pulls (4)	2¼″ dia. x 1¼″

HARDWARE

#12 x 1¾″ Roundhead wood screws (16)
#12 Flat washers (16)
#10 x 1½″ Flathead wood screws (4)

1 ***Cut all parts to size.*** To build this project, you will need approximately 22 board feet of 8/4 (eight-quarters) stock, 4 board feet of 4/4 (four-quarters) stock, and one-quarter sheet (2′ x 4′) of ¼″ plywood. Plane 20 board feet of the 8/4 stock to 1¼″ thick to make the top, supports, and guides. Plane the remaining 2 board feet to 1¾″ thick to make the legs. Plane all of the 4/4 stock to ¾″ thick to make the drawer parts.

Glue up the wide stock needed for the top. Turning cubes for drawer pulls, 2½″ to a side, must also be glued up.

Cut all the parts, with the exception of the legs and the drawer pulls, to the sizes shown in the Materials List. Cut the legs approximately 2″ longer than specified so that you have a little extra stock to help mount them on the lathe. Don't cut the drawer pull stock at all; wait until after you've turned the pulls.

2 ***Make the supports.*** Drill 1¼″-diameter holes in the supports to hold the legs, as shown in the *Support Layout*. These holes must be drilled at a *compound* angle, so that the legs angle toward the corners of the bench, not simply toward the ends or sides.

Tilt your drill press worktable to 10¼°, front-to-back. Mark three lines on your worktable; they must intersect where the tip of the drill bit touches the table. The first line must be perpendicular to the table's front edge. The next two must be at 45° angles to the first line. To avoid marking on the worktable, put down strips of tape. (See Figure 1.) Clamp the support stock to the worktable, parallel with the *left* 45° line, and drill one of the round mortises. (See Figure 2.) Turn the support end for end, and reclamp it to the worktable, parallel to the *right* 45° line, and drill the second hole. Repeat this procedure for the other support.

Note: Because the support holes are drilled at a compound angle, the legs will appear to splay at 10°, not 10¼°, when viewed from the side or the front. This angle is *not* critical, so don't worry about adjusting your drill press worktable precisely. As long as you drill the hole at slightly more than 10°, the table should sit properly.

After you create the round mortises, make pilot holes for the screws that will secure the supports to the top. These pilot holes are really *slots,* so that the top can expand and contract with changes in the weather. To make them, first drill a ¾″-diameter counterbore, ½″ deep. Inside the counterbore, drill a line of three 3/16″-diameter holes through the stock. Remove the waste between the holes by angling the drill bit back and forth. The long dimension of the slots should be parallel to the grain direction of the supports, which will put them perpendicular to the grain of the top in the finished assembly.

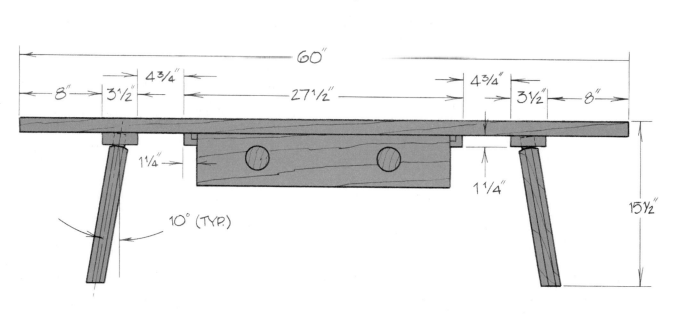

FRONT VIEW

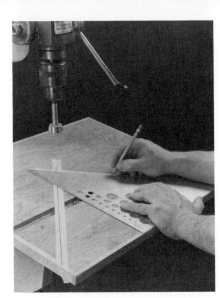

1/Mark your lines on the worktable with masking tape. That way, you can just peel them up when you're finished drilling the round mortises.

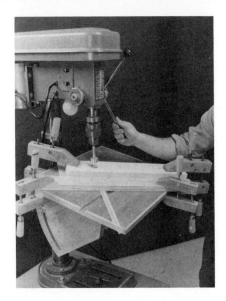

2/The support will tend to creep as you drill, no matter how securely you clamp it. To prevent this, clamp a straightedge to the worktable and butt the workpiece against it.

3 Make the drawer guides.

Since the drawer guides are attached to the top in the same manner as the supports, make the guides next. With a table saw or a router, cut a ½″-wide, ⁹/₁₆″-deep rabbet along one edge of each guide, as shown in the *Guide Detail*. Then drill pilot slots for screws, exactly as you did in the supports. Remember, the long dimension of the slots should be parallel to the grain direction of the guides.

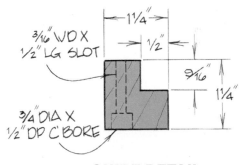

³/₁₆″ WD X ½″ LG SLOT

1¼″

½″

⁹/₁₆

1¼″

³/₄″ DIA X ½″ DP C'BORE

GUIDE DETAIL

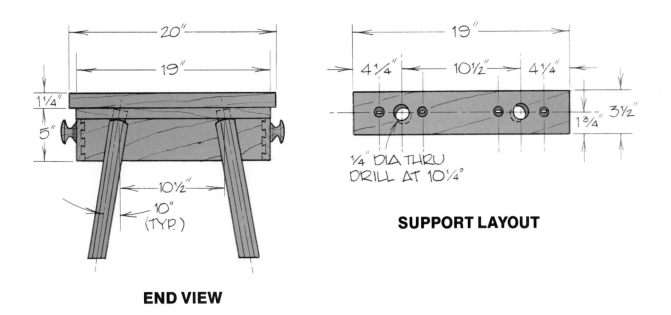

20″

19″

1¼″

5″

10½″

10° (TYP.)

END VIEW

19″

4¼″   10½″   4¼″

3½″

1¾″

¼″ DIA THRU DRILL AT 10¼°

SUPPORT LAYOUT

4 Make the legs.

Make the legs. Bevel-rip the legs to an octagonal shape, using a table saw with the blade tilted at 45°. (See Figure 3.) If you have a hollow-ground planer blade, use it to make these cuts. This blade will leave a smooth surface, requiring little additional work. If you use an ordinary blade, smooth the cut surfaces with a jointer or a sander. (See Figure 4.)

Mount the legs on a lathe, and turn the tenons on the upper ends. Be very careful to make these tenons exactly 1¼″ in diameter so that they will fit snugly in the supports. If they are even slightly undersized, the bench will be weakened.

After making the tenons, cut the legs to the proper length. Miter the bottom of the legs at 10¼°, to match the angle of the holes. Once again, this angle is not critical. Just make sure that the angle is slightly more than 10°, and that all four legs are precisely the same length.

3/Bevel-rip the square leg stock to make it octagonal. Cut test pieces until you get the rip fence positioned so that all eight sides of the octagon will be equal. Then rip the four corners of each leg without moving the fence. (Sawguard removed for clarity.)

*4/If you smooth the octagonal legs on a jointer, tilt the fence at a 45° angle **away** from the knives. This will provide a "cradle" for the stock as you joint it.*

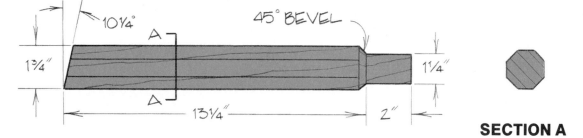

10¼°   45° BEVEL

A

1¾″

A

13¼″   2″   1¼″

LEG DETAIL

SECTION A

TRY THIS! To ensure that the tenons fit properly in the supports, make a tenon gauge. Using the same bit you used to drill the round mortises, drill two holes in a scrap of plywood. With a saw, open up one hole to an outside edge, and cut a 1/16″ step in the gauge, as shown in the illustration. As you turn, use this gauge to measure the diameter. When you can slip the gauge over the tenon up to the step, you know that you are approaching the correct diameter. Make very light cuts until the gauge slips completely over the tenon. Confirm the fit by removing the leg from the lathe and inserting the tenon in the other (closed) hole in the gauge.

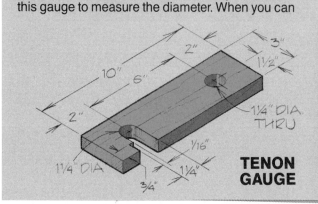

3″
1½″
2″
10″
6″
1¼″ DIA THRU
2″
1/16″
1¼″ DIA
1¼″
3/4″

TENON GAUGE

5 **_Turn the drawer pulls._** While you're set up for lathe work, make the four drawer pulls. These are *faceplate* turnings. Glue each of the turning blocks to a scrap of ¾"-thick wood, with a sheet of paper in between the blocks and the scraps. Glue the end grain of the turning block to the face of the scrap. Mount each block on the lathe by driving screws through the faceplate and into the scrap. Turn the pull as shown in the *Drawer Pull Detail*. Finish sand the turning. Separate the pull from the scrap by placing a chisel at the seam between the two pieces of wood and striking it sharply with a mallet. Because of the paper in the glue joint, the pull and the scrap will part cleanly and easily.

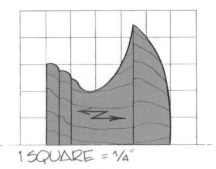

1 SQUARE = ¼"

DRAWER PULL DETAIL

Note: The grain of the pull should run parallel to the turning axis. It's very difficult to turn the stock otherwise.

6 **_Cut the drawer joinery._** The sides of the drawer are attached to the front and the back by half-blind dovetails, as shown in the *Drawer/End View*. The drawer bottom rests in a ¼"-wide, ⅜"-deep groove in the side of the drawer sides, front, and back. The easiest way, perhaps, to make all of this joinery is with a router. Use a dovetail bit and a dovetail template to cut the dovetails, then cut the drawer bottom grooves with a straight bit. Countersink and drill 3/16"-diameter pilot holes in the front and the back to mount the drawer pulls.

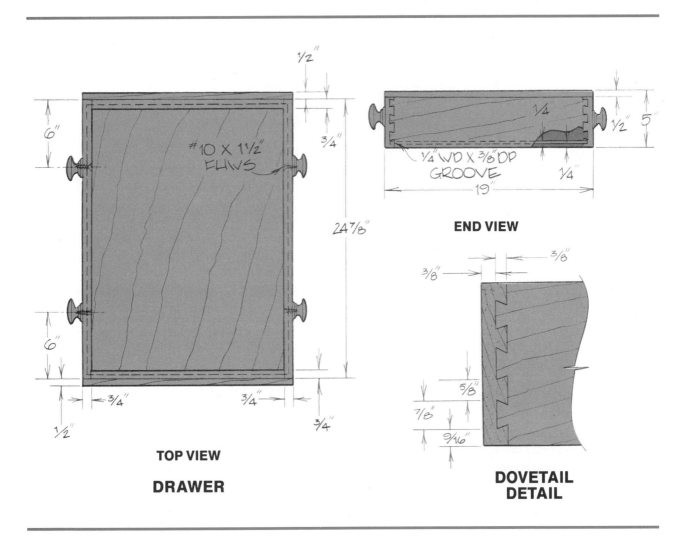

#10 X 1½" FHWS

¼" WD X ⅜" DP GROOVE

END VIEW

TOP VIEW

DRAWER

DOVETAIL DETAIL

7 **Assemble the drawer parts.** Finish sand all the parts that you have made (except for the pulls — these have already been sanded). Be careful not to round over any edges or corners that adjoin other parts.

Assemble the drawer. Glue the sides to the front and the back. Do not apply any glue to the bottom; let it float in its groove. After the glue dries, lightly sand the dovetail joints so that all surfaces are flush. Then glue the drawer glides to the drawer sides, flush with the upper edges. Secure the pulls to the front and back of the drawer with #10 x 1½" flathead wood screws.

8 **Assemble the bench.** While the glue cures on the drawer, attach the supports to the top with #12 x 1¾" roundhead wood screws and flat washers, where shown in the *Front View*. Do *not* glue the parts together. That would prevent the top from shrinking and swelling properly, and the top would ultimately warp or cup. Tighten the screws so that they are snug, but not so tight that the washers bite into the wood.

Next, *temporarily* fit the legs into the supports. Turn the bench right side up, resting on its legs on a *flat* surface. Check that the bottoms of all four legs rest flat on this surface. If they don't, turn them until they do. Turn the bench upside down and mark the positions of the legs in the round mortises. Remove the legs, apply glue to the tenons, and fit them in place permanently.

#12 X 1¾"
RHWS W/#12 WASHER

3/16 WD X ½ LG SLOT

¾ DIA X ½ DP C'BORE

TOP-TO-SUPPORT JOINERY DETAIL

9 **Install the drawer.** With the bench upside down, set the drawer in place. Place the drawer guides over the glides, and clamp them to the top. There should be a ¹/₁₆"-wide gap (approximately) between the outside edge of the glides and the inside edge of the guides. Test the action of the drawer, ensuring that it will open from either side of the bench. (You can do this with the bench upside down.) Adjust the position of the guides until the drawer slides smoothly without binding. Then attach the guides to the top with roundhead screws and washers, as you did the supports.

10 **Finish the bench.** Slide the drawer out of its guides. Do any necessary touch-up sanding, and apply a finish to the completed bench. If you use a finish that builds up on the surface of the wood, such as varnish or shellac, do *not* apply it to the guide or glide surfaces that rub together. Finish these surfaces with an oil, such as tung oil or Danish oil, that soaks into the wood. After the finish dries, rub the drawer glides with paraffin.

Game Board

Board games were an important pastime for country folks. Almost every country home had at least one game board; most had several.

The boards were often reversible, with a different game on each side. This checkerboard has a Parcheesi layout on the back. They were usually painted in bright colors and sometimes were decorated with carvings or moldings. In some cases, the pieces were painted so that you could play a third game. For example, the topsides of the checkers might be painted with symbols for kings, queens, knights, bishops, and so on, so that the pieces could also be used to play chess.

The games they played were much the same as those we play today — chess, checkers, Parcheesi, backgammon, and so on. There were some subtle differences, however. The spaces on a Parcheesi board or the bars on a backgammon board often differed from one region to another. Checkerboards sometimes had more squares on them than we're used to seeing. The checkerboard that you see here, for instance, has 12 squares to a side. The number of pieces were the same — each player had 12 checkers — but the checkers were arranged at the beginning of the game with gaps among the ranks of the pieces. Opponents thus had more room to maneuver, and better strategy was required to win. These 10- and 12-square checkerboards were sometimes referred to as Canadian checkerboards, since they were most popular in the northern states and Canada. ✸

Materials List

FINISHED DIMENSIONS

PARTS

A. Board   ¾″ x 18″ x 24″

B. Side trim (2)   ¼″ x 1¼″ x 24½″

C. End trim (2)   ¼″ x 1¼″ x 18½″

D. Dividers (4)   ¼″ x ½″ x 18″

E. Checkers (24)   1½″ dia. x ⅜″

F. Parcheesi
markers (16)   ¾″ x ¾″ x 1¼″

G. Dice (2)   ¾″ x ¾″ x ¾″

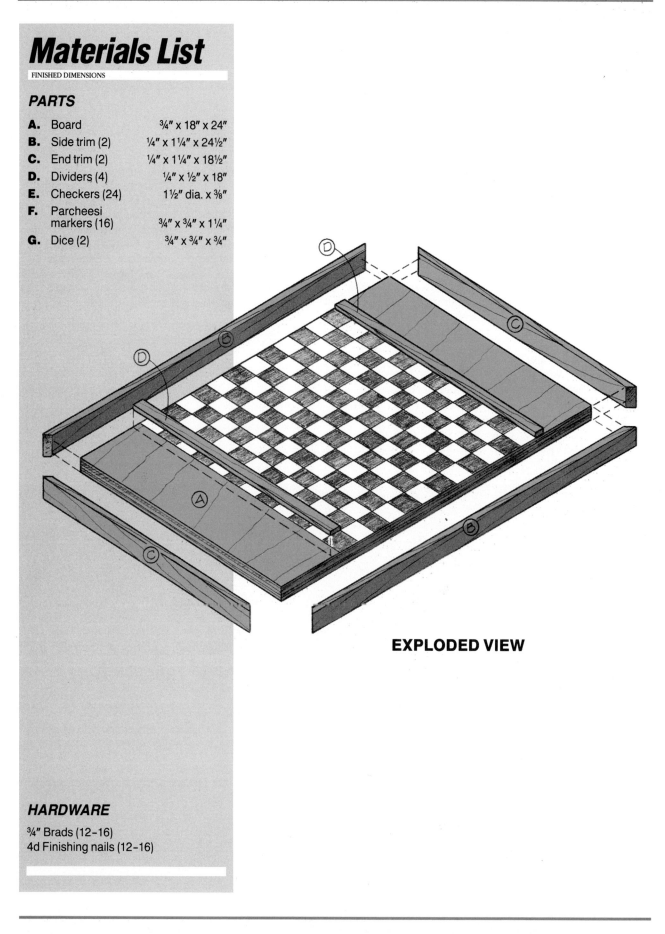

EXPLODED VIEW

HARDWARE

¾″ Brads (12–16)
4d Finishing nails (12–16)

1

Cut all parts to size. As you can see by the Materials List, this game board requires few materials. You can make one out of scrap wood. Since the finished project will be painted, you don't have to use expensive wood. We recommend, however, that you use ¾″ plywood for the board itself. (You can use solid wood for the trim and the dividers.)

Plywood is very stable — that is, it doesn't change shape with changes in humidity and temperature. A piece of solid wood 18″ thick will expand and contract up to ⅜″ *across* the grain — more than enough to pop the miter joints between the trim parts at the corners of the board. A wide piece of solid wood also may warp or twist.

Once you have selected the materials, cut the parts to the sizes shown on the Materials List. Miter the ends of the trim as shown in the drawings of *Side 1* and *Side 2*.

2

If necessary, fill the voids in the ply-wood. Depending on the grade of plywood that you use, you may have to fill the voids on one side of the plywood. Properly filled, the voids won't detract from the finished project. Once you paint the game board, no one will be able to tell where the voids were. Use a two-part, resin-based, waterproof wood putty, such as Minwax's High Performance Wood Filler, to fill these voids. (Ordinary water- and acetone-based putty chips easily and may disintegrate if the game board gets wet.)

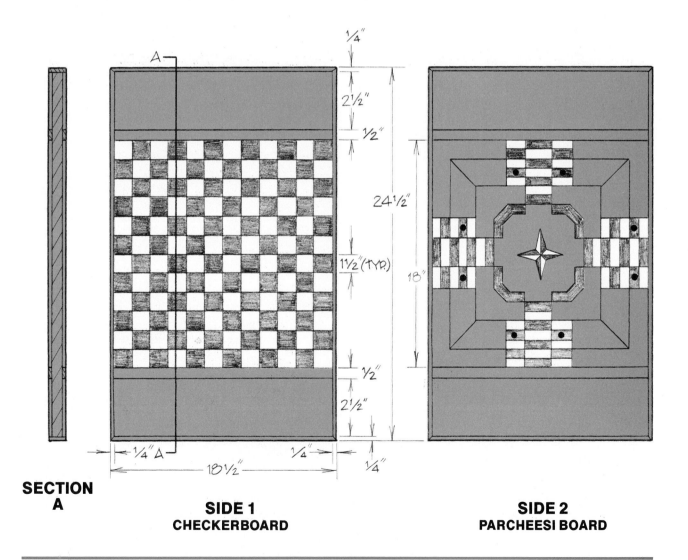

SECTION A

SIDE 1
CHECKERBOARD

SIDE 2
PARCHEESI BOARD

3 **Sand the parts.** Sand and smooth the board, the dividers, and the *inside* face of the trim parts *before* you assemble the game board. Be careful to keep the surface of the board flat and even. (If you have filled any voids, the soft plywood will sand away much easier than the putty, leaving a wavy surface.) Also be careful not to round over any edges or corners that adjoin other parts.

4 **Assemble the game board.** Glue the trim and the dividers to the board, tacking them in place with brads. The trim should form a lip around the edge of the board, as shown in the *Joinery Detail*. Once the glue dries, set the heads of the brads just below the surface of the wood. Cover the heads with wood putty.

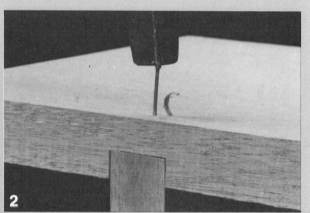

JOINERY DETAIL

TRY THIS! If you wish to finish the trim rather than paint it, you may want to use a more sophisticated method for hiding the heads of the brads. Using a special blind-nail plane, lift a small curl of wood where you want to position the nail. *Do not* separate the curl from the stock. Drive a nail where you have lifted the curl and set the head. Put a little glue on the back of the curl and press it back in place. Hold the curl down with tape until the glue dries. When you remove the tape, you won't be able to tell there's a nail just under the surface of the wood. Blind-nail planes are available from many woodworking specialty supply houses.

5 Round the edges of the assembly.

Using coarse sandpaper, round over the hard edges of the trim and the dividers to give the completed game board a worn look. Finish sand the outside face of the trim, and do any necessary touch-up sanding on the rest of the board.

6 Paint the completed board.

Lay out the checkerboard on one side of the board and the Parcheesi game on the other. The checkerboard is just a grid of squares. Use 1½″ squares if you want to duplicate the 12-square Canadian playing field shown here, and 2¼″ squares if you want to make a traditional 8-square playing field. The Parcheesi playing field is slightly more complicated. Refer to the *Parcheesi Playing Field Layout* for precise measurements and patterns.

Paint the playing fields in bright colors. Use acrylic paint: It's easy to work with, you can mix any color that you want, and it's waterproof after it dries. Use any color scheme that strikes your fancy — there were no traditional colors for the playing fields among country folk. They often painted these boards in red, white, and blue — a patriotic motif — but they used other colors, too.

After the paint dries, give it a light sanding. If you want the board to look very old and well-used, sand the parts of the board that would have received the most wear, partially exposing the wood. Then apply a coat of burnt umber glaze. Rub most of the glaze off before it dries completely. This will give the board an antique appearance. (Glazes are available at most craft and hobby supply stores.)

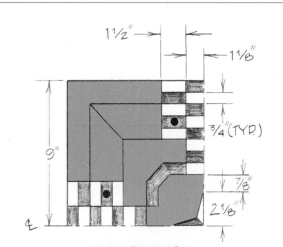

**PARCHEESI
PLAYING FIELD LAYOUT**

7 Make the playing pieces.

The checkers can be cut from a length of closet pole. Or you can turn a 1½″-diameter cylinder on your lathe. Slice this cylinder (or pole) into ⅜″-thick wafers. Sand the wafers, then paint them. Once again, you don't have to use any particular colors — so long as you use two different colors.

Cut small, rectangular pieces of wood ¾″ thick, ¾″ wide, and 1¼″ long to make the Parcheesi markers.

You'll need 16 markers in all. Sand these pieces and paint them. Use four different colors, producing four pieces of each color.

If you wish, you can also make your own dice. Cut two cubes of hardwood, ¾″ to a side. Sand the faces and carefully round over the edges, so that the dice will tumble easily when they are rolled. Paint dots or numerals on the faces of the dice.

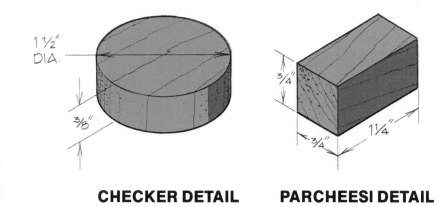

CHECKER DETAIL   **PARCHEESI DETAIL**   **DIE DETAIL**

Lap Desk

Despite the name, lap desks were rarely used on laps. When they first appeared in medieval Europe, they were intended to be set on a table or small stand. They weren't always used as desks. In colonial America, they were more often used to store the family Bible, birth certificates, and other important papers. Country folk called them "Bible boxes." Today, these boxes make wonderful catch-alls.

The lap desk (or Bible box, if you prefer) is a simple form — a box with a sloping lid. Many lap desks incorporate partitions and small drawers to help organize papers and writing materials. The desk shown has two drawers. One pulls out from the right side of the box to become an inkwell. The other drawer, intended to hold pens, nibs, and writing paraphernalia, opens inside the box.

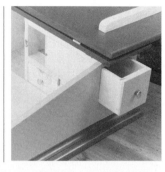

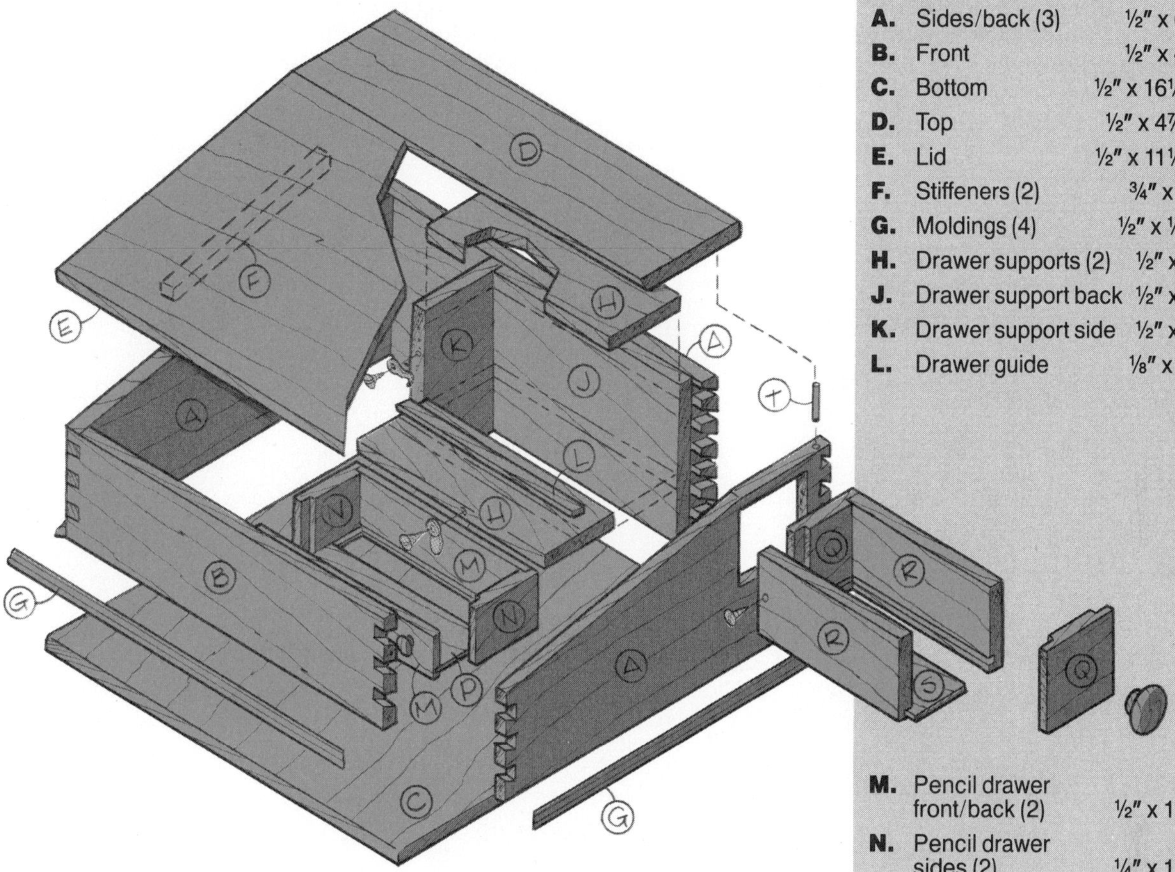

EXPLODED VIEW

Materials List

FINISHED DIMENSIONS

PARTS

A.	Sides/back (3)	½" x 6" x 14½"
B.	Front	½" x 4" x 14½"
C.	Bottom	½" x 16¼" x 16¼"
D.	Top	½" x 4⅞" x 16¼"
E.	Lid	½" x 11½" x 16¼"
F.	Stiffeners (2)	¾" x ¾" x 7¼"
G.	Moldings (4)	½" x ½" x 15½"
H.	Drawer supports (2)	½" x 3" x 8½"
J.	Drawer support back	½" x 6" x 8½"
K.	Drawer support side	½" x 3½" x 6"
L.	Drawer guide	⅛" x ½" x 8½"

M.	Pencil drawer front/back (2)	½" x 1⅞" x 8⅜"
N.	Pencil drawer sides (2)	¼" x 1⅞" x 2½"
P.	Pencil drawer bottom	⅛" x 2¼" x 8⅛"
Q.	Inkwell drawer front/back (2)	½" x 2⅞" x 2⅞"
R.	Inkwell drawer sides (2)	¼" x 2⅞" x 8½"
S.	Inkwell drawer bottom	⅛" x 2⅝" x 8¼"
T.	Dowels (3)	¼" dia." x ¾"

HARDWARE

#8 x 1" Roundhead wood screws (15)
#8 Flat washers (15)
1" Brads (25–30)
Decorative hinges and mounting
　screws (1 pair)
Small drawer pulls (3)
Small hook
Small turnbutton
#4 x ½" Roundhead wood screws (3)

1 **Cut the parts to size.** You can make this lap desk from approximately 8 board feet of lumber. Plane most of it to ½″ thick. Plane a small amount (less than a board foot each) of ¾″-thick stock (for the stiffeners), ¼″-thick stock (for the drawer sides), and ⅛″-thick stock (for the drawer bottoms).

After you have planed the stock to the proper thicknesses, glue up the wide stock you need to make the bottom and the lid. With a couple of exceptions, cut the parts to the sizes shown in the Materials List. The exceptions are the moldings — you'll make these later on — and the front. Rip the front to the 6″ width of the sides and the back to simplify cutting the dovetails that join these four parts. Remember to bevel the adjoining edges of the lid and the top, as shown in the *Side View.*

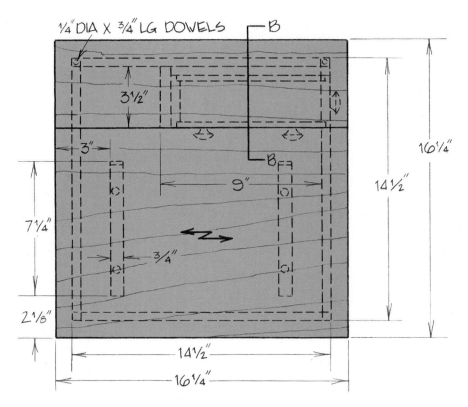

TOP VIEW

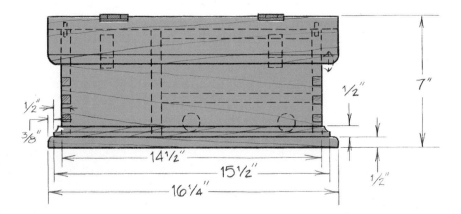

FRONT VIEW

2 Cut the dovetails in the front, back, and sides.

Cut the dovetails in the front, back, and sides. As shown in the *Front View* and the *Side View*, the front, back, and sides of the lap desk are joined with dovetails. If you have a router and a dovetail jig, rout the dovetails. You can also cut the dovetail joints by hand.

Country craftsmen traditionally used dovetails in making small boxes and chests. While they look nice, the dovetails are not essential. The *Alternate Corner Joinery* drawings show two other possibilities — splined miter joints and finger joints. Use an ordinary combination blade in a table saw to cut the slots for the splines in the miters. Make the finger joints with a table saw equipped with a dado cutter.

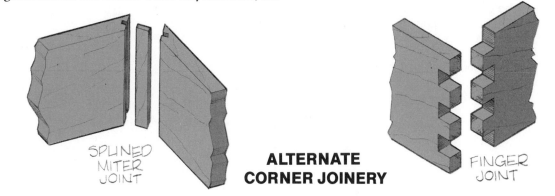

SPLINED MITER JOINT

ALTERNATE CORNER JOINERY

FINGER JOINT

3 Trim the sides and the front to final size.

Trim the sides and the front to final size. Temporarily assemble the front, back, and sides. Carefully lay out the taper on each side and bevel on the front. On the right side, mark the cutout for the inkwell drawer, as shown in the *Side View*. Disassemble the parts, and cut the sides with a table saw and a tapering jig. Rip the front to the proper width, beveling the edge at 10°.

Cut out the opening for the inkwell drawer in the right side with a saber saw or a scroll saw. To do this, drill a small hole, approximately ⅜" in diameter, inside the "waste." Insert the blade through the hole, and cut to the inside of your lines. Later, as you assemble the lap desk, you can square up the cutout with a file.

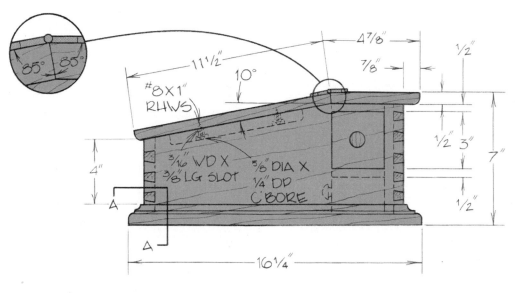

SIDE VIEW

4

Assemble the drawer support. Finish sand the drawer supports, drawer support back, drawer support side, and drawer guide. Assemble the parts with glue and brads. Be sure the assembly is square. Set the heads of the brads after the glue dries.

5

Shape the edges of the bottom, top, and lid. Using a ¼"-radius quarter-round bit in your router or shaper, dress the edges of the bottom, top, and the lid, as shown in the *Front View, Side View,* and *Section A. Do not* round over the beveled edges of the top or the lid.

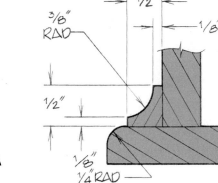

SECTION A

6

Finish sand the parts of the lap desk. Finish sand the parts you have made so far — bottom, top, lid, sides, front, and back. Sand only the faces, not the edges, and be careful not to round over any corners.

7

Assemble the front, back, sides, and bottom. Once again, *temporarily* assemble the sides, front, and back. Set this assembly on the bottom piece, center it, and lightly mark its position in pencil. Also set the drawer support assembly in place, and outline the drawer support side on the bottom.

The bottom is attached to the lap desk with round-head screws in *slots*. The purpose of these slots is to allow the bottom to expand and contract without distorting the case. To make these slots, first drill ⅝"-diameter, ¼"-deep counterbores in the underside of the bottom, as shown in the *Bottom Layout*. Inside these counterbores, create the slots by drilling two ³⁄₁₆"-diameter holes side by side, then angling the drill bit back and forth to remove the waste between the holes. Remember: The slots must be *perpendicular* to the wood grain so the bottom can move properly.

Glue the sides, front, and back together, making sure the assembly is square. After the glue dries, do any necessary touch-up sanding at the corners, then attach the bottom to this assembly. Use no glue, only #8 x 1" roundhead wood screws and flat washers. Tighten the screws snugly, but not so much that the washers bite into the wood. If the screws are too tight, the bottom won't be able to shrink and swell.

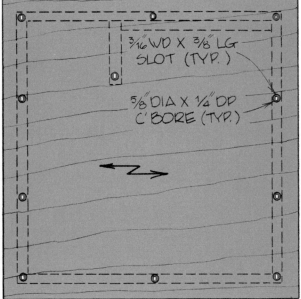

BOTTOM LAYOUT
BOTTOM VIEW

8 Attach the drawer support to the lap desk.

Apply glue to the drawer support assembly where it will contact the back and side of the lap desk, then set it in place. *Do not* glue the drawer support assembly to the lap desk bottom. As mentioned, the bottom must remain free to expand and contract.

After the glue dries, drive brads through the lap desk sides into the ends of the drawer supports, reinforcing the joints. Drive a roundhead screw through the last slot in the bottom and into the drawer support side. With a file, square up the inkwell drawer opening in the lap desk side, filing the edges flush with the surfaces of the drawer support assembly.

TRY THIS! If you don't want the heads of the brads to be visible on the outside of your lap desk, use a blind nail plane to lift a curl of wood wherever you want to drive a brad. Glue the curl of wood back in place after you set the brad.

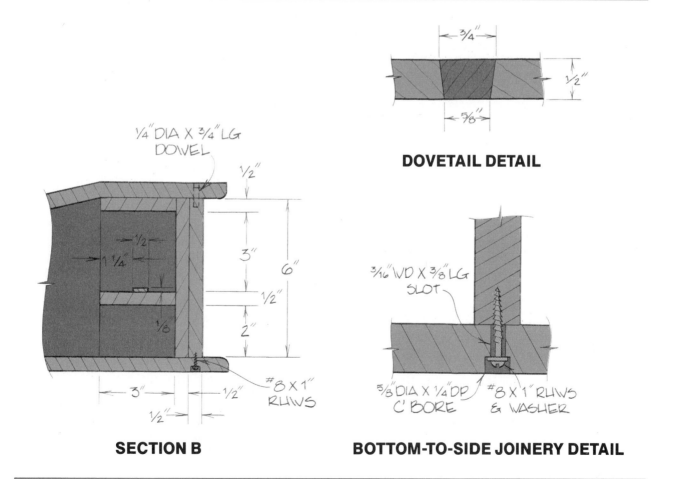

DOVETAIL DETAIL

SECTION B

BOTTOM-TO-SIDE JOINERY DETAIL

9 **Attach the top and the lid.** If necessary, sand or file the top surfaces of the lap desk and drawer support to make them flush. Drill stopped holes, ¼″ in diameter and ½″ deep, in the top edges, as shown in the *Top View.* Put dowel centers in these holes, then lay the top in position. Press it firmly onto the centers, marking the locations for matching dowel holes. (See Figure 1.)

Drill the stopped holes, ¼″ in diameter and ¼″ deep, in the top. Then glue the top to the lap desk and the drawer support, using ¼″-diameter, ¾″-long dowels to reinforce the glue joints.

While the glue is drying, attach the stiffeners to the lid. These stiffeners keep the lid from warping, while allowing it to expand and contract. Counterbore and drill slots in the stiffeners, just as you did in the bottom. Then drive screws through the slots and into the underside of the lid. *Do not* glue the stiffeners to the lid.

1/Use dowel centers to match up dowel holes in the lap desk assembly and its top. A center will make a small indentation in wood pressed onto it. To make the indentation more visible, rub a pencil on the center's point before you press the wood onto it.

Remember that the slots must be perpendicular to the grain of the lid. After the stiffeners are in place, hinge the lid to the top.

10 **Build and fit the drawers.** Cut ¼″-wide, ¼″-deep rabbets in the edges of the drawer fronts and backs, and ⅛″-wide, ⅛″-deep grooves in the drawer sides, fronts, and backs. Also make a ⁷⁄₁₆″-wide, ⅛″-deep notch centered in the bottom edge of the inkwell drawer back. The positions of these joints are shown in the *Inkwell Drawer* and *Pencil Drawer* drawings.

Finish sand the drawer parts. Then assemble them with glue and brads. *Do not* glue or nail the bottoms in the drawers; let them float in their grooves. After the glue dries, install drawer pulls, and fit the drawers to their respective openings. The notch in the back of the inkwell drawer should fit over the drawer guide. If necessary, sand or plane stock from the edges and faces of the drawers until the drawers slide smoothly.

TRY THIS! Build the drawers ¹⁄₁₆″–⅛″ oversize from the dimensions shown in the Materials List, then sand away the excess stock after the drawers are built. This way, you can get a perfect fit.

Install a small turnbutton on the lower drawer support to keep the pencil drawer closed. On the drawer support side and the back of the inkwell drawer, install a small hook and a #4 roundhead wood screw. The hook and screw will keep the inkwell drawer closed, and the screw will also serve as a stop to keep the drawer from sliding completely out of the lap desk.

11 **Make and attach the moldings.** Using a router or shaper, cut a ⅜″-radius cove in the edge of a ½″-thick board at least 18″ long. Rip the shaped edge free of the board (see Figure 2), then repeat, creating five or six molding strips. The extra moldings are insurance — in case you chip one or cut it too short.

Carefully measure the sides, front, and back of the lap desk where you intend to install the moldings. Because of the repeated sanding, the dimensions may not exactly match what's shown on the Materials List. Cut the moldings to fit, mitering the ends at 45°. Then attach them to the sides, front, and back with glue and brads. *Do not* glue or nail them to the bottom; remember, it must be free to expand and contract.

2/When making small moldings, always cut the shape in a wide board, then rip the molding free. Never try to shape narrow stock because it may break up and injure you.

12 Finish the completed lap desk.

Remove all the hardware — hinges, pulls, hooks, and screws — *except* for the screws that hold the bottom in place. Do any necessary touch-up sanding, and apply a finish. If you use a finish that builds up on the surface, such as varnish or paint, do not apply it where the drawers and drawer supports touch. Use a *penetrating* finish on these areas so the drawers will continue to work properly. The lap desk shown is painted, but the inside is "stained" with *diluted* paint — paint thinned so it soaks into the wood surface, rather than building up on top of it.

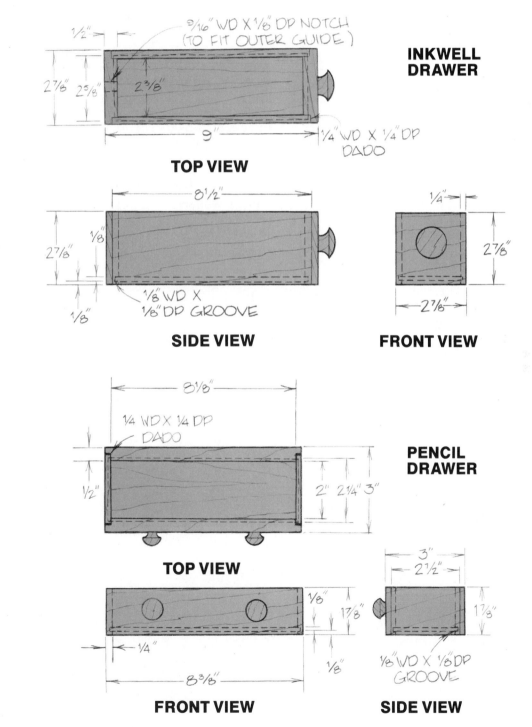

Windsor Settee

The country settee, the forerunner of our modern sofa, was simply a chair stretched sideways to accommodate two or more people. They were most often built in the Windsor style, distinguished by delicate legs, stretchers, and spindles.

The origin of the Windsor style is lost, but there is an interesting (although unfounded) folktale about how it was discovered. The story goes that one day in the mid-seventeenth century, the Duke of Windsor was out riding in his woods. He came upon a bodger — an itinerant chairmaker — who had set up his portable pole-lathe near a grove of young trees. The Duke inspected an example of the bodger's work, and found it much more delicate and well-made than the ordinary country chair. He was also astonished to find that a piece so delicate could be so sturdy. He ordered a set of chairs from the bodger and proudly displayed them at the next ducal dinner. His guests naturally admired the bodger's work, and they soon were ordering their own "Windsor" chairs.

This particular Windsor settee is, perhaps, the last word in delicate. It was made by Robert Pinter, a modern-day country craftsman, who carefully copied it from a nineteenth-century antique in the Philadelphia Museum of Art. Pinter is a professional furnituremaker in Tipp City, Ohio, specializing in traditional furniture. The original was built by a Shaker brother in Enfield, New Hampshire. This brother dispensed with traditional bracework, apparently considering it unnecessary. By choosing his materials and his joints carefully, he created a piece that has been sturdy enough to last almost two hundred years.

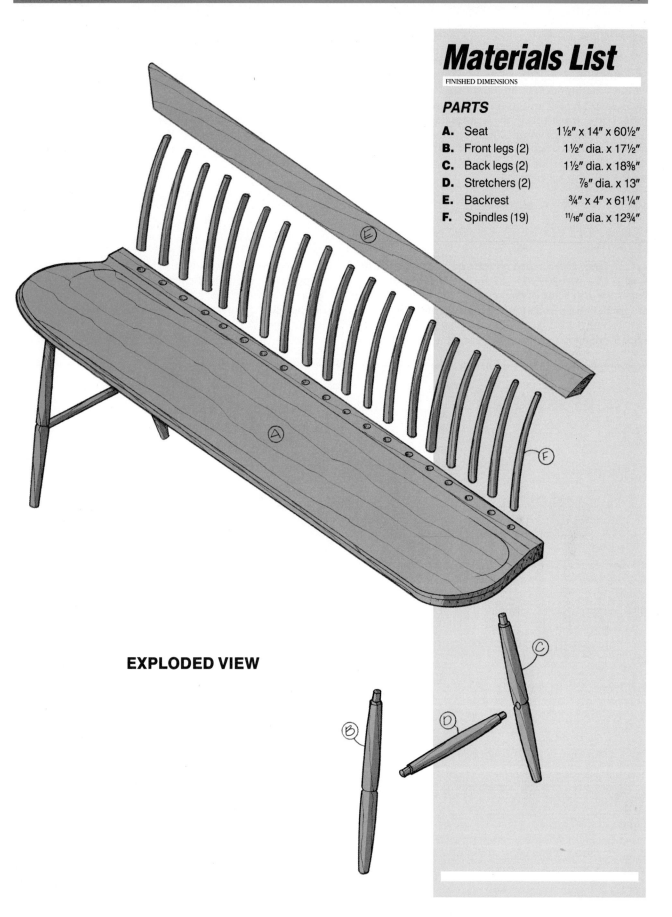

Materials List

FINISHED DIMENSIONS

PARTS

A.	Seat	1½″ x 14″ x 60½″
B.	Front legs (2)	1½″ dia. x 17½″
C.	Back legs (2)	1½″ dia. x 18⅜″
D.	Stretchers (2)	⅞″ dia. x 13″
E.	Backrest	¾″ x 4″ x 61¼″
F.	Spindles (19)	¹¹⁄₁₆″ dia. x 12¾″

EXPLODED VIEW

1

Select and prepare the stock.   To make this settee, you'll need approximately 12 board feet of a medium-soft to medium-hard wood for the seat, and 6 board feet of an extremely hard wood to make the other parts. Traditionally, the seats of these settees were made from eastern white pine and all the other parts from rock maple. The settee shown here has a poplar seat, rock maple spindles, and figured maple legs, stretchers, and backrest.

Plane the seat stock to 1½″ thick, and cut it to the size shown in the Materials List. Cut the backrest stock to its proper width. "Skim" it in the planer to remove the rough surface, but don't take it down to its final thickness just yet. Cut the rest of the stock into the turning spindles you need. To make it easier to turn, each spindle should be 1″–2″ longer than the dimension indicated in the Materials List.

2

Drill the round mortises in the seat and the backrest.   In the bottom edge of the backrest, drill a line of nineteen ⅜″-diameter, ¾″-deep stopped holes, 3″ on center. In the top of the seat, 1⅛″ in from the back edge, drill a matching line of ½″-diameter, 1″-deep stopped holes, angled at 5° toward the back.

Turn the seat over and drill 1″-diameter, 1″-deep stopped holes to hold the legs, as shown in the *Front View* and *Seat Profile*. As indicated, the front holes must be angled at 2° toward the front and the back holes toward the back at 15°.

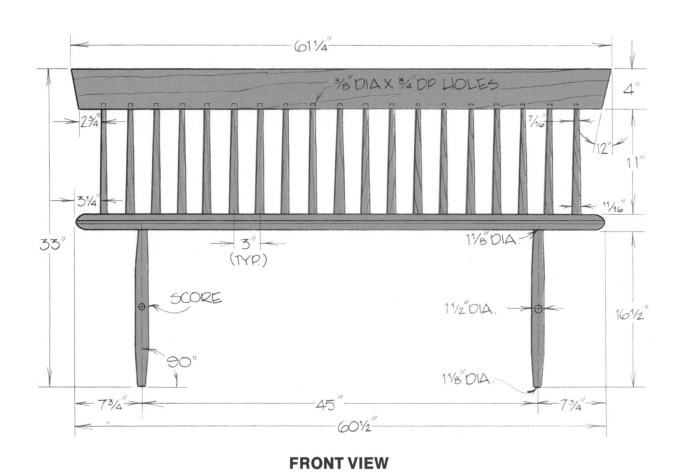

FRONT VIEW

3 **Shape the seat.** Enlarge the *Seat Profile* and *Seat Shape* patterns. Trace the profile on the seat, but hold off on the shape until after you've scooped out the seat. Trace a profile on *both* ends of the board to make it easier to refer to it as you work.

Shaping the settee seat involves extensive handwork, but some tasks can be done on power tools. First, bevel-rip chamfers on the bottom front and bottom back edges. Cut the front chamfer at 45°, and the back at 20°. Then hollow out as much of the top surface of the seat as you can, making overlapping cove cuts with a radial arm or table saw. (See Figure 1.)

1/Rough out the seat depression by making overlapping cove cuts with a saw. Feed the seat across the blade at a 45° angle. Take small bites, cutting just ¹⁄₁₆" deeper with each pass until the cove reaches the depth shown in the Seat Profile.

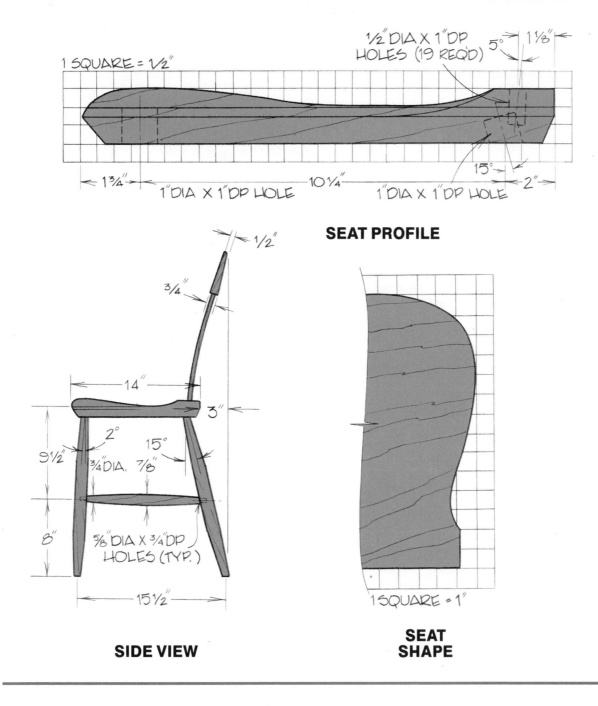

SEAT PROFILE

SIDE VIEW

SEAT SHAPE

Trace the seat shape onto each end of the seat stock, and cut the shape with a saber saw. Now the handwork begins. Plane, rasp, file, scrape, and sand the stock until the seat reaches the final contours shown in the drawings. It helps to clamp a long, straight board to the top surface. The front edge of this board should be 1¾″ from the back edge of the seat. (See Figure 2.) This board helps to preserve a hard line between the flat and the curved areas of the seat. Without the board, you might round over this line while scraping and sanding. A subtle but nonetheless critical element of the design would be lost.

2/While you're shaping the seat, preserve the hard line between the flat and the curved areas by clamping a board along the line. Sand and scrape the flat area *first*.

4 **Resaw and resurface the backrest.**　To taper the backrest, resaw one face on a band saw with the table tilted 5°. Smooth the resawed face on your jointer. Joint the top edge with the fence of the jointer tilted 2½° away from the knives, and the bottom edge with it tilted 2½° toward the knives.

TRY THIS!　If you have a 4″ jointer, you know it's very difficult to surface a 4″-wide board. The knives have to be set exactly right. Save yourself considerable trouble by cutting the backrest ⅛″–¼″ narrower than specified, making it no more than 3⅞″ wide.

5 **Turn the legs, stretchers, and spindles.**　Turn all the round parts — legs, stretchers, and spindles — on a lathe. Use a steadyrest to keep the parts from whipping as you turn them. Be especially careful when making the tenons on these parts — they must fit the round mortises precisely. A loose joint will be weak, and it will grow weaker each time you sit on the settee.

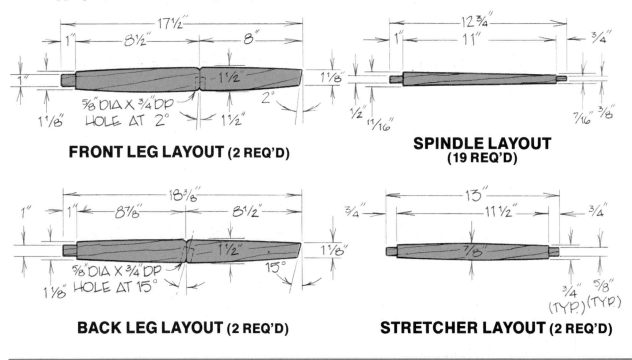

FRONT LEG LAYOUT (2 REQ'D)

SPINDLE LAYOUT (19 REQ'D)

BACK LEG LAYOUT (2 REQ'D)

STRETCHER LAYOUT (2 REQ'D)

To help achieve the proper diameters, make several gauges. Drill a hole in a scrap of wood using the same bit you used to bore the mortises. Cut a slot from the outside edge of the scrap into the hole. Carefully rasp away the edges of the slot until the slot is *precisely* as wide as the tenons you want to make. Turn each tenon until it is *slightly* larger than the desired diameter. Hold the tenon gauge against the tenon from one side, while you sand the tenon from the other. (See Figure 3.) When the gauge slips over the tenon, stop sanding *immediately* — the tenon diameter is correct.

When turning the legs, lightly score them with the point of a skew chisel, as shown in the *Front View* and the *Side View*. These shallow grooves are not only decorative, they mark the location of the mortises for the stretchers.

As you finish each turning, finish sand it on the lathe. To get the smoothest possible surface, work with progressively finer grits until you reach 150# sandpaper.

3/Sandpaper removes stock more slowly than a chisel, so use it to remove the last little bit of stock from the tenon. There's less chance of accidentally making the tenons too small. As you work, use a home-made tenon gauge to ensure you achieve the precise size of the tenon needed.

Then turn off the motor and sand the part *with* the grain.

Cut the turned parts to the proper lengths. Cut the bottoms of the front legs at 2°, the back legs at 15°.

---

6 **Drill mortises for the stretchers.** Insert the legs temporarily into the seat, making a bench, and set the seat on a flat surface. Turn the legs so that the ends rest flat on the surface. Mark the *inside* of each leg at the centerline so that you know where to drill the mortises for the stretchers.

To immobilize a leg while you drill, put it in a V-jig. Since it is tapered, the ends must be shimmed. Drill a ⅝″-diameter, ¾″-deep stopped hole in each leg at the mark. Angle the holes in the front legs at 2°, and the back legs at 15°.

---

7 **Bend the spindles.** On this bench, the spindles are bent so the back arches gracefully. Consider this arch *optional* — many Windsor settees were built with straight spindles. To produce the arch, you must bend all 19 spindles.

To do this, first make a bending jig. Enlarge the curve shown in the *Bending Jig Pattern* and trace it on a large, thick board. (We used 3″ x 4″ x 12″ block, glued up from ¾″ plywood scraps.) Cut the curve with a band

saw so that the board falls apart in two halves. Using a gouge, carve 4-5 semi-round grooves along the sawn surface of each half of the jig. The grooves in the two parts should line up, as shown in the *Bending Jig/ End View*.

Note: Carving these grooves is time consuming, but without them, the bending jig will press a flat area on the front and back of each spindle. The flats are almost impossible to sand out, so the grooves are important.

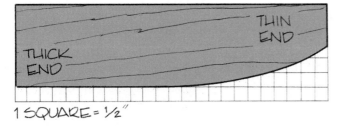

THIN END

THICK END

1 SQUARE = ½″

BENDING JIG PATTERN

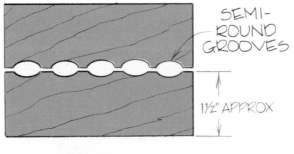

SEMI-ROUND GROOVES

1½" APPROX

BENDING JIG
END VIEW

Boil 4-5 spindles (one for each set of grooves) in a large pan for 45-50 minutes. Lay them in the grooves of one-half of the jig with their thin ends where the jig's curve is most pronounced. Fit the jig's second half on top, and clamp the halves together, bending the spindles. (See Figure 4.) You have to do this fairly quickly, before the wood cools. Keep the spindles clamped in the jig for at least a week. Repeat the process weekly until you have bent all the spindles.

Don't be alarmed if, when you remove the spindles from the jig, they straighten slightly. Wood normally loses about 20% of its curve after it's steam-bent. The jig's curve has been calculated to account for this. After taking the spindles out of the jig, scrape and sand them smooth — the water will have raised the grain.

4/Place the tapered ends over the portion of the jig where the curve is more pronounced. The slender parts of the spindles will bend easier than the thicker parts.

8 ***Assemble the settee.*** Finish sand all the parts that still need it. Then dry assemble the bench to ensure that everything fits properly. If it does, reassemble the settee with glue. Use plenty of glue and wipe away the excess with a wet rag. This will raise the grain slightly, making it necessary for you to do a little touch-up sanding after the glue dries. But the sanding is less work than removing glue beads with a chisel.

9 ***Finish the settee.*** Carefully check all surfaces and lightly sand where needed. Then apply a finish to the completed project. Traditionally, settees were painted. Some, however, were finished with clear shellacs and varnishes, particularly those built of figured wood. If you apply a clear finish, use something very durable, such as spar varnish or polyurethane. Wipe on very thin coats with a clean rag. This will make it easier to rub down the turned parts between each coat.

Turning Figured Wood

*M*any classic country pieces were turned from figured woods — crotches, burls, and stock with curly grain. These woods are striking, but they require great patience and care to turn them properly.

The secret is twofold. First, your chisels must be razor sharp. Hone them before you begin, and re-hone them frequently as you work. Second, you must cut or *shear* the wood, not scrape it. If you scrape, the chisel will tear the grain and ruin the stock. Set the height of the tool rest even with the top of the turning. Hold the chisel so that it shaves the stock as it revolves on the lathe. (See Figure A.) The cutting edge should be at a slight angle to the turning axis, as you look at the stock from the top.

If you hold the chisel just right, the tool shears and *burnishes* the wood. The cutting edge slices a paper-thin curl from the stock, and the flat area immediately behind the edge presses the wood fibers back in place, preventing any tear-out. This burnishing also brings out the figuring. This will take practice, but the results are worth the effort.

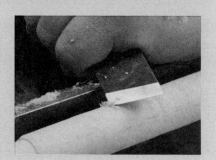

A/Be careful to keep the point of the chisel up so that it doesn't accidentally dig into the wood.

Weathervanes

W hen farming is your livelihood, you need to know what the weather will be from day to day. With no weather forecasts to rely on, early settlers watched the wind. They knew that the direction of the wind could indicate weather changes. Wind from the southwest often brought warm, pleasant conditions; wind from the northeast brought cold and misery. A sudden change in the wind sometimes preceded violent storms. Every barn, church, and public building was equipped with a weathervane so that folks knew what to expect.

Many of the old weathervanes were quite fanciful. The "windcock" — the part of the vane that points into the wind — was often carved or painted to represent an animal, person, or mythological figure. Now prized as folk art, many old-time weathervanes are displayed indoors as primitive sculptures or conversation pieces.

The weathervanes shown can be used indoors or out. Made almost entirely from wood (as many early country weathervanes were), they will work outdoors every bit as well as metal vanes. Indoors, they can be displayed two different ways. If you have the room, you can display the entire vane, compass points and all. If space is tight, display the windcock alone.

Materials List

FINISHED DIMENSIONS

PARTS

A. Horse windcock   ¾″ x 11″ x 21¼″

B. Rooster
windcock   ¾″ x 10⅞″ x 13⅜″

C. Compass points "E",
"N", and "S" (3)   ¾″ x 3¼″ x 3½″

D. Compass
point "W"   ¾″ x 3½″ x 4½″

E. Scrolls (8)   ¾″ x 2⅜″ x 3½″

F. Pivot dowel   ¾″ dia. x 12¼″*

G. "E" and "W"
dowels (2)   ½″ dia. x 6″

H. "N" dowel   ½″ dia. x 5¾″

J. "S" dowel   ½″ dia. x 6⅞″

K. Scroll dowels (4)   ¼″ dia. x 2″

L. Compass disk   6″ dia. x ¾″

M. Stand (for horse
windcock)   11″ dia. x ¾″

N. Stand (for rooster
windcock)   8″ dia. x ¾″

HARDWARE

¼″ dia. x 2¼″ Steel rod
12d Common nail

*The pivot dowel can be shortened to
3″ if you wish to make a windcock and
display it without the compass points.*

EXPLODED VIEW

1

Prepare the stock. Many of this project's parts — the windcocks, the compass letters, and the scrolls — are intricate. Take this into account as you choose your stock. If made from solid wood, these parts will have spots prone to break easily. For example, the horse will surely snap where the leg mounts the pivot if laid out with the grain running lengthwise through the body. But cutting these parts from commercial plywood may be no better alternative. Voids will need to be filled, and the plies will intrude through however many layers of paint you apply, detracting from the project's appearance.

The best compromise is to make your own ¾″-thick plywood using ¼″-thick boards. Laminate three such boards, using a generous amount of glue to get a good bond. The grain of the middle ply should run perpendicular to that of the other two. Make the outer layers from single boards at least 11″ wide and as long as you need them, then make up the inner layer from shorter boards laid edge to edge. (They should be as long as the outer layers are wide.) For the horse, compass point, and scrolls, make a plywood board 11¼″ wide and 34″ long. For the chicken, compass points, and scrolls, you'll need a board 11″ wide and 24″ long.

Note: If you're going to display this project outside, choose a wood that isn't too fragile but weathers well. Avoid redwood, pine, and treated lumber. Mahogany is your best choice, followed by poplar and Atlantic white cedar (juniper). Use a waterproof glue such as resorcinol to laminate the plies and assemble the project.

SIDE VIEW

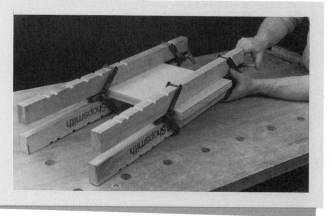

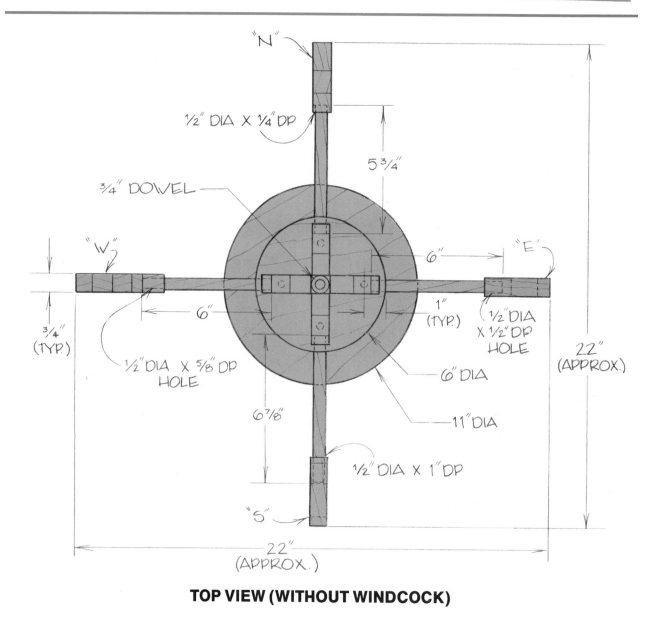

"N"

½" DIA X ¼" DP

5 ¾"

¾" DOWEL

6"

"E"

"W"

6"

1" (TYP.)

½" DIA X ½" DP HOLE

¾" (TYP.)

½" DIA X ⅝" DP HOLE

6" DIA

22" (APPROX.)

6 ⅞"

11" DIA

½" DIA X 1" DP

"S"

22" (APPROX.)

TOP VIEW (WITHOUT WINDCOCK)

2 *Trace the patterns on the stock.*

Enlarge the patterns of the shaped parts. Trace these patterns on the stock you made. Lay out the circular parts you need — compass disk and stand — on ¾"-thick solid stock using a compass.

Note: There are a lot of intricate patterns in this project. To save yourself time, have a copying or duplicating business with a *variable* enlarging/reducing copier enlarge the patterns for you. These machines aren't precise, but a little inprecision won't matter.

1 SQUARE = ½"

PATTERNS

3

Cut the shapes of the parts. With a band saw or a scroll saw, cut out the windcock, compass points, scrolls, disks, and stand. Remove the saw marks from the edges with files and sandpaper.

TRY THIS! If you have a choice between a band saw and a scroll saw, choose the scroll saw. Look for a woodcutting blade with more teeth per inch than any other and use it to make the cuts. (Don't use metal-cutting blades.) A fine scroll saw blade leaves a smooth edge, and there will be little sanding to do.

4

Cut the dowels to length and drill the holes. The remaining parts are all lengths of dowel. Cut them to the lengths specified on the Materials List.

The parts of the weathervane are assembled with these dowels, so the joinery is a simple matter of drilling holes. Some of these holes, however, must be drilled in irregularly shaped parts. You must use ingenuity to get the job done. Make the jig shown in the *Drilling Jig Detail* to hold the letters and the scrolls. (See Figures 1 and 2.) Make a V-jig to hold the compass disk. (See Figure 3.) To drill the pivot hole in the windcock and the pivot dowel, tilt the drill press table so the work surface is parallel to the drill bit and clamp the workpiece to the table. (See Figure 4.)

In addition, there are some holes that can be made without special setups. Drill a ¾″-diameter hole through

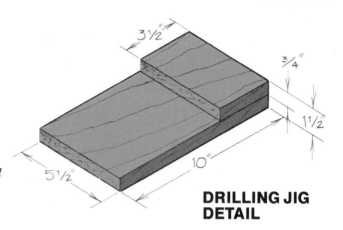

DRILLING JIG DETAIL

the center of the compass disk and a ¾″-diameter, ½″-deep stopped hole in the center of the stand for the pivot dowel. Drill four ¼″-diameter holes through the compass disk for the scroll dowels, as shown in the *Top View*.

1/To drill the ¼″-diameter, ⅝″-deep stopped holes in the scrolls, clamp the drilling jig to the drill press fence, then clamp a scroll in the jig so the inside edge is against the step, and the bottom edge is flush with the top of the jig.

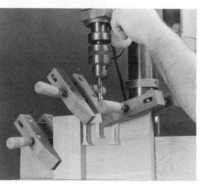

2/When drilling the ½″-diameter stopped hole in a compass point, align it in the jig so that the bottom of the letter rests against the step of the jig.

3/To drill the ½″-diameter, ½″-deep stopped holes in the edge of the compass disc, clamp a V-jig to the drill press fence in the same way you attached the drilling jig. Position the jig so the crotch of the "V" is directly beneath the drill bit.

4/To bore the ¼″-diameter, 1″-deep stopped pivot hole in the windcock, tilt the entire drill press worktable and clamp the stock to it. Place a sheet of sandpaper, folded in half, between the table and the stock to keep it from creeping down as you drill.

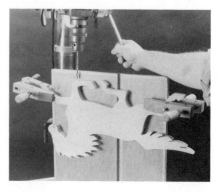

5

Make the pivot.   Cut a 2¼″-long piece of ¼″-diameter steel rod to make the pivot point. Clamp the rod in the chuck of your hand-held power drill. Set up a stationary belt, disk, or strip sander — it doesn't matter which — and turn it on. Squeeze the drill's trigger and gingerly hold the end of the rod, at an angle, against the belt or disk. Make sure the drill spins

against the direction of the sander. In a short time, the opposing actions will grind a point on the end of the rod. (See Figure 5.)

In addition to a point, you also need a metal surface at the bottom of the pivot hole in the windcock. Otherwise the sharp point will bite into the soft wood like a nail, boring the hole deeper and deeper. To make this surface, cut the head off a 12d common nail. Using a hammer and a punch, drive the head into the bottom of the pivot hole, as shown in the *Pivot Detail*. When assembled, the pivot point will press against the head of the nail.

5/When grinding metal with a sander, use a worn-out disk or belt. You'll have better control, there will be less flying debris, the ground surface will be smoother, and you won't ruin good sanding disks or belts.

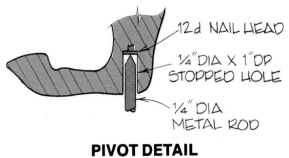

PIVOT DETAIL

6

Assemble the weathervane.   Dry assemble the weathervane. When you're satisfied the parts fit together properly, take the weathervane apart and finish sand all the surfaces that need it. Then reassemble the wooden parts with glue.

The metal pivot will probably fit much too tightly in the pivot hole. To loosen it without making it wobbly, press a little wax into the hole. Mount the pivot rod in the chuck of a hand-held power drill, and insert the rod

in the pivot hole. Turn on the drill, and let the rod spin at a medium speed for 10-15 seconds. Check the pivoting action. If it's still tight, repeat until the windcock turns freely.

Press the pivot, point up, into the pivot dowel. Place the windcock on the pivot. There should be approximately ¼″ of space between the end of the pivot dowel and the bottom of the windcock.

7

Paint the weathervane.   Remove the windcock from the pivot and do any necessary touch-up sanding on the completed project. Cover the pivot rod with masking tape, then paint the project. If you're going to display the weathervane outdoors, use exterior paints. If it is to be kept indoors, you can use

almost any paint or stain that suits your fancy. Our weathervanes are painted with traditional milk paints, then covered with a dark (burnt umber) glaze to give them an old, weathered look. Both milk paint and glazes are available at most craft and hobby stores.

Audio/Video "Kas"

Most country homes were built without closets. They made home building more complex, and added material and expense. Consequently, closets were a luxury. Instead of closets, country folk stored their clothes in large cabinets. The eighteenth-century English settler called his cabinet a "wardrobe" or "linen press." In the early nineteenth century, waves of Scandinavian settlers brought their own version of the cabinet, a *"kas."*

Today, closets are commonplace. A large cabinet like this can serve another purpose. In the living room or den, it can be an excellent *entertainment center.* It is large enough to hold a wide variety of audio and video equipment. The cabinet shown has been modified slightly to accommodate a 26″ television, a VCR, a stereo receiver, tape and disk player.

Because the cabinet was so large, the country craftsman designed it to be taken apart and moved easily. The front, back, sides, top, and bottom were joined by pegged mortises and tenons. When the pegs were knocked out, the cabinet came apart.

This modern *kas* is made in a similar way. It's assembled with knockdown fasteners called trapeze fittings. It comes apart into six major sections, plus doors and

shelves. Even the drawer assembly is a separate unit. It rests on the bottom of the *kas.*

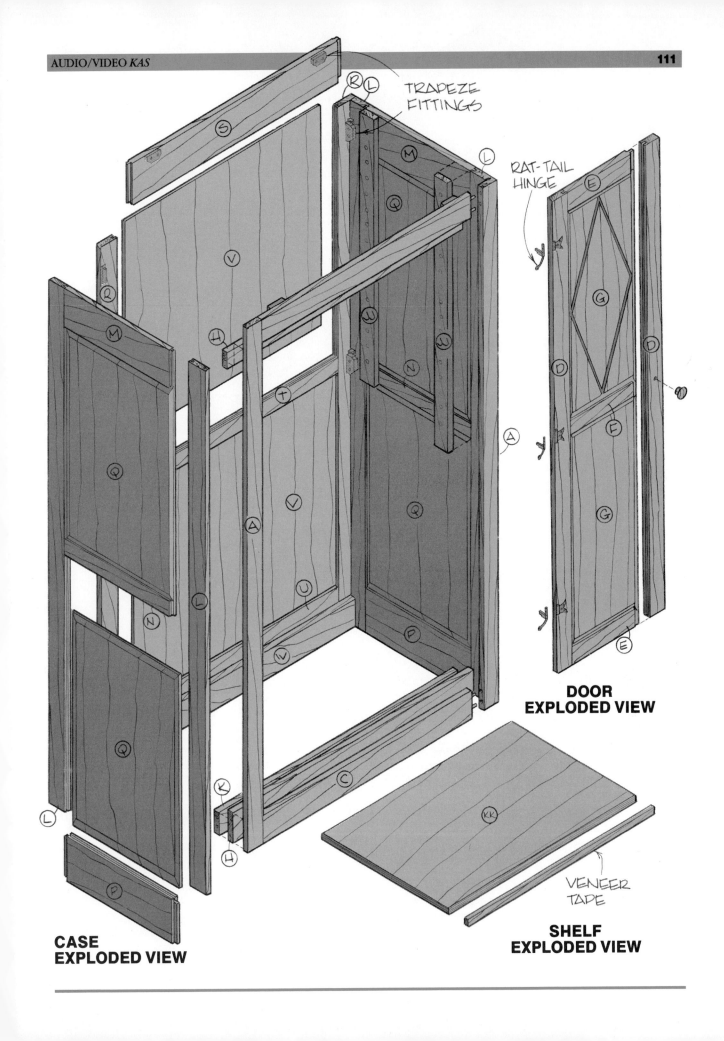

TRAPEZE FITTINGS

RAT-TAIL HINGE

DOOR EXPLODED VIEW

VENEER TAPE

SHELF EXPLODED VIEW

CASE EXPLODED VIEW

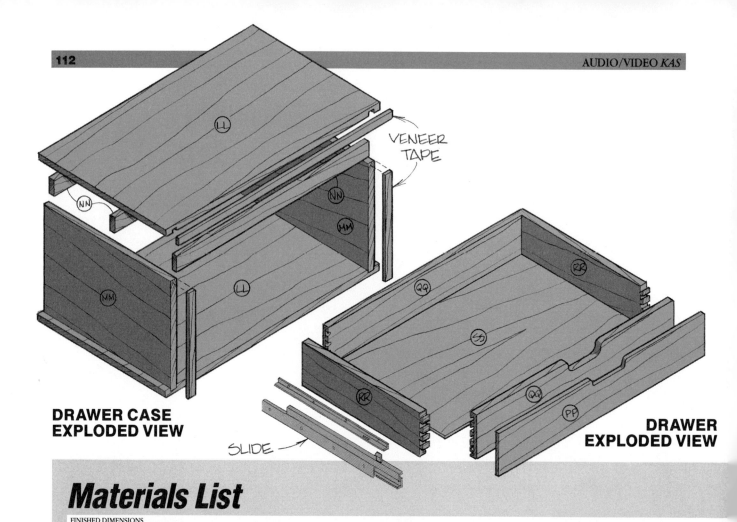

**DRAWER CASE
EXPLODED VIEW**

VENEER TAPE

SLIDE

**DRAWER
EXPLODED VIEW**

Materials List

FINISHED DIMENSIONS

PARTS

Front Frame and Doors

A.	Front frame stiles (2)	¾″ x 2½″ x 68½″
B.	Front frame top rail	¾″ x 3″ x 29½″
C.	Front frame bottom rail	¾″ x 3½″ x 29½″
D.	Door frame stiles (4)	¾″ x 2¼″ x 61⅞″
E.	Door frame top/ bottom rails (4)	¾″ x 2¼″ x 11⅛″
F.	Door frame middle rails (2)	¾″ x 2″ x 11⅛″
G.	Door panels (4)	¾″ x 10⅞″ x 28⁷⁄₁₆″
H.	Upper door stop	¾″ x 2″ x 33″
J.	Lower door stop	¾″ x 4″ x 33″
K.	Bottom rest	¾″ x 2¾″ x 33″

Sides

L.	Side frame stiles (4)	¾″ x 2¼″ x 68½″
M.	Side frame top rails (2)	¾″ x 5¼″ x 17½″
N.	Side frame middle rails (2)	¾″ x 2″ x 17½″
P.	Side frame bottom rails (2)	¾″ x 5¾″ x 17½″
Q.	Side panels (4)	¾″ x 17¼″ x 28½″

Back

R.	Back frame stiles (2)	¾″ x 2½″ x 68½″
S.	Back frame top rail	¾″ x 5¼″ x 30½″
T.	Back frame middle rail	¾″ x 2″ x 30½″
U.	Back frame bottom rail	¾″ x 5¾″ x 30½″
V.	Back panels* (2)	¼″ x 28¾″ x 30½″
W.	Bottom rest	¾″ x 2¾″ x 33″

Top

X.	Top*	¾″ x 23⅝″ x 36¾″
Y.	Top cove molding (total)	¾″ x 2″ x 84″
Z.	Top bead molding (total)	¾″ x 3¼″ x 87″
AA.	Top crown molding (total)	¾″ x 3⁹⁄₁₆″ x 97″
BB.	Top stop molding (total)	½″ x 1″ x 98″
CC.	Glue blocks (13)	¾″ x 1¹¹⁄₁₆″ x 1¹¹⁄₁₆″

Bottom

DD.	Bottom*	¾″ x 23⅝″ x 36¾″
EE.	Bottom cove molding (total)	¾″ x 2½″ x 84″
FF.	Bottom bead molding (total)	¾″ x 6¾″ x 87″
GG.	Back support	¾″ x 4¼″ x 36″
HH.	Glue blocks (4)	¾″ x ¾″ x 4¼″

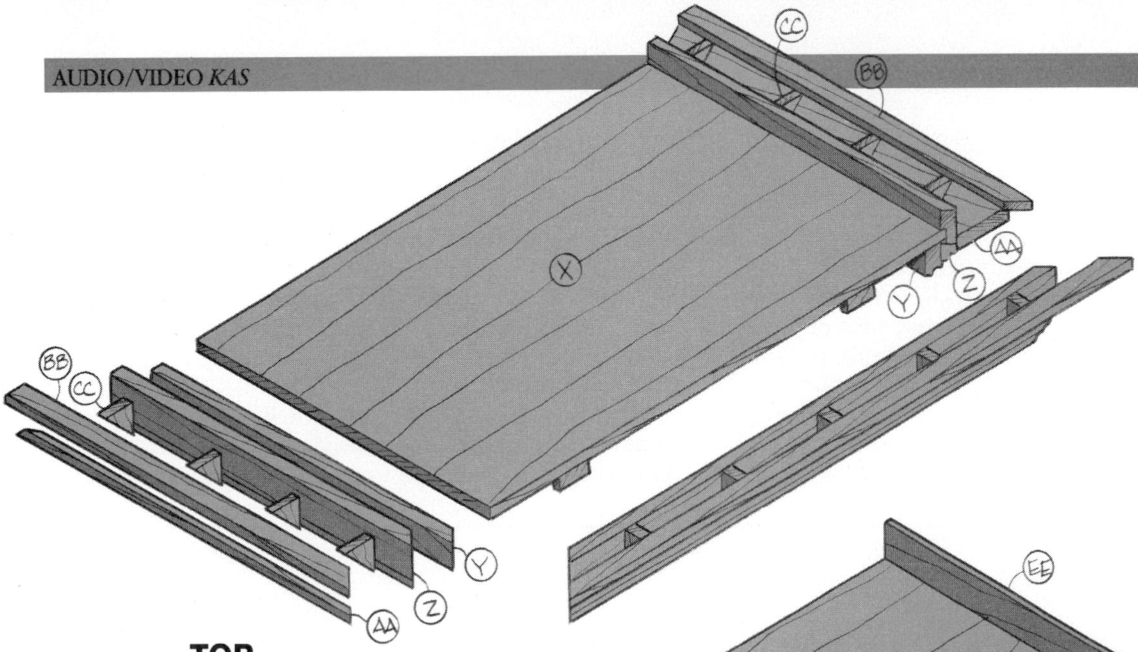

**TOP
EXPLODED VIEW**

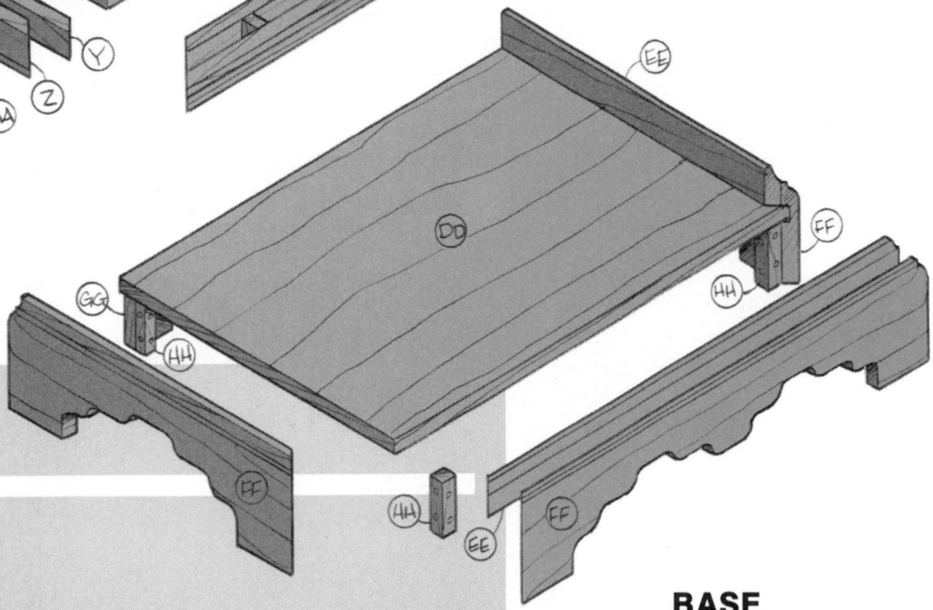

**BASE
EXPLODED VIEW**

Shelves and Drawers

JJ. Shelving
supports (2)   ¾" x 2" x 35"

KK. Adjustable
shelves*
(3–4)   ¾" x 20¼" x 31⅜"

LL. Drawer unit
top/bottom* (2)   ¾" x 20¼" x 33"

MM. Drawer
supports* (2)   ¾" x 14¾" x 20¼"

NN. Braces (3)   ¾" x 2" x 29½"

PP. Drawer
faces (2)   ⅜" x 5⅞" x 29⅜"

QQ. Drawer
fronts/backs   ¾" x 5⅞" x 28½"

RR. Drawer
sides (4)   ¾" x 5⅞" x 19⅛"

SS. Drawer
bottoms* (2)   ¼" x 19⅛" x 27¾"

*These parts can be made from
plywood.*

HARDWARE

Trapeze knock-down fasteners (14)
#10 x 1¼" Flathead wood screws
  (36–48)
⅝" Wire brads (96–108)
Rat-tail hinges and mounting screws
  (3 pairs)
Door pulls (2)
Door catches (4)
#20 Plates (6–8)*
20" Full-extension drawer slides and
  mounting screws (2 pairs)
TV pullout/swivel (optional)
Pin-style shelving supports (12–16)
Veneer tape (optional)

*You may substitute ⅜"-diameter,
2"-long dowels instead of the #20
plates.*

1 *Cut the parts for the front, side, and back sections.*

The Scandinavian country craftsman who built a *kas* like this usually painted it with bright colors. If you intend to paint yours, you won't need to buy expensive lumber. Use either white pine or poplar — the *kas* you see here was made with both, and some plywood as well. You can use a good deal of plywood. The adjustable shelves, drawer unit, and back panels are all made of it. Just trim the exposed edges with veneer tape or thin strips of solid wood to hide the plies.

To build the *kas,* you'll need approximately 76 board feet of 4/4 (four quarters) stock, 1½ sheets (4' x 8' and 4' x 4') of ¾" cabinet-grade plywood, and 1 sheet (4' x 8') of ¼" cabinet-grade plywood. Plane all of the solid stock to ¾" thick. Rip several long strips — enough to make the top stop molding — to 1" wide, then plane these to ½" thick.

Warning: If you plan to paint the *kas,* you may be tempted to purchase inexpensive #1 or #2 construction-grade yellow pine. *Don't.* Construction-grade lumber is

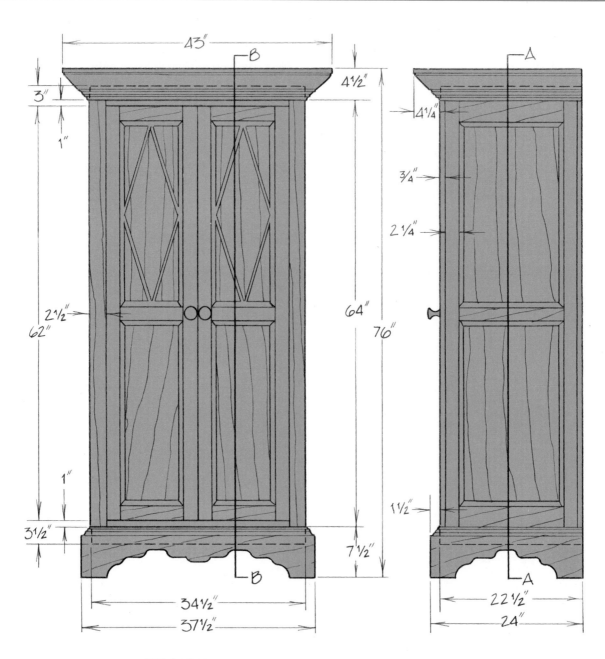

FRONT VIEW   **SIDE VIEW**

dried to 30% moisture content. It will lose more moisture after you use it, and the parts of the project may warp and twist — even though the wood is clear! Cabinet-grade lumber has been dried to 7%-8% moisture content, and is very stable. The chances that it will distort are negligible.

Glue up the wide stock for the door and side panels. Then cut all the parts for the front, side, and back sections to the sizes shown in the Materials List. It's best not to cut the parts for the top, bottom, shelving, and drawer until you've built the first four sections. It will be hard enough to keep track of the parts for the front, sides, and back — the other parts will just clutter your shop. Moreover, woodworking projects — large projects, in particular — have a way of changing size and shape slightly as you build them. You may need to adjust the dimensions of the top, bottom, shelves, and drawers slightly to fit the first four sections you build.

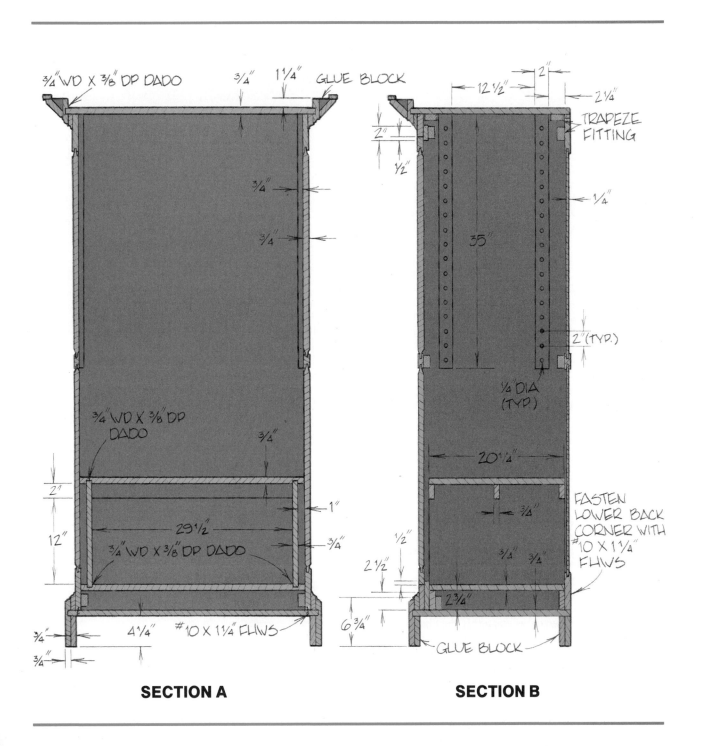

SECTION A   **SECTION B**

2

Cut the tongues and grooves. The door, side, and back frames are all assembled with tongue and groove joints, as shown in the *Frame Joinery Detail*. The easiest tool to use to cut this many tongues and grooves is a table saw with a dado cutter. You can also use a router, but it will take longer.

Cut the grooves first. Make them ¼″ wide and ½″ deep on the *inside* edges of all the rails and stiles. Cut them in *both* edges of the middle stiles. Then cut the tongues to fit the grooves. Adjust the dado cutter to make a ½″-wide, ¼″-deep rabbet. Cut a rabbet on one side of a board, then flip it face for face, and cut the other side — the two rabbets will form a tongue. (See Figure 1.) Cut tongues in the ends of all the rails.

1/When you cut the tongues, guide the rails across the dado cutter with a miter gauge. Use the fence as a stop, so the tongues can't be cut more than ½″ long. Use a miter gauge extension that reaches almost to the fence to help keep the ends of the rail from binding and kicking back.

TRY THIS! Cut a tongue in a piece of scrap and test its fit in a groove *before* you cut good wood.

3

Cut the raised panels. Several tools cut raised panels — the table saw, the shaper, and the router. We have designed these panels to be cut in two passes, using a table saw-mounted dado cutter and a router.

Without changing the setup used to cut the tongues, cut ¼″-wide, ½″-long tongues on all the edges of the door and side panels. Secure a ⅜″-radius *unpiloted* cove bit in a table-mounted router. (Most cove bits have removable pilots.) Adjust the height of the bit so that it will touch — but not cut — the tongues. Clamp a fence or a straightedge to the table to guide the work. Then cut a cove in both shoulders of all the tongues. (See Figure 2.)

Note: It's not absolutely necessary to cut both the inside and the outside shoulders, but it does make the panel reversible. Choose the best-looking side after you raise the panels, and face it out.

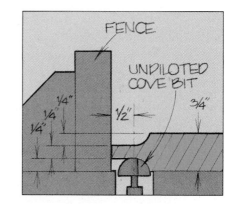

2/When you cut the raised panels, the cove bit should protrude ¼″ above the table, and the fence should be ½″ from the center of the bit.

Using a ½″ core-box bit, rout round-bottomed grooves in the upper door panels, making the diamond shapes shown in the *Front View*. Clamp a straightedge to the panel to guide the router, then cut one side of one diamond. Reposition the straightedge and repeat until you have completed both diamonds.

4

Assemble the doors, sides, and back. Finish sand all the rails, stiles, and panels. Drill a hole for electrical cords in the lower back panel. Assemble the frames with glue, inserting the panels in the grooves. Do *not* glue them in the frames. Let them float.

Note: It is extremely important that all the frames be as square as you can make them. Check them carefully with a carpenter's square as you apply the clamps.

When the glue dries, attach the bottom rest to the back frame with flathead wood screws. Place the rest flush with the bottom edge of the bottom rail, centered on the frame. Its ends should be ¾″ shy of the outside edges of the frame.

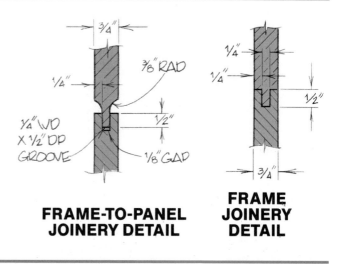

FRAME-TO-PANEL JOINERY DETAIL

FRAME JOINERY DETAIL

5

Join the parts of the front frame.

Assemble the rails and stiles of the front frame with either dowel or plate joints. Butt the parts together, end to edge, and mark across each joint with a pencil. Use the pencil marks to locate the holes for the dowels or the slots for the plates. Drill the dowel holes with the aid of a doweling jig, or use a plate joiner to cut the slots. (See Figure 3.)

Finish sand the parts of the front frame and assemble them with glue. When the glue dries, attach the top door stop, bottom door stop, and bottom rest to the inside of the frame with flathead wood screws. Each of these parts should be centered on the frame, like the rest attached to the back frame. The door stops should protrude ½″

3/If you join the parts of the front frame with plates, cut a double row of splines for added strength.

into the opening, as shown in *Section B*. Position the bottom stop and the bottom rest flush with the bottom rail.

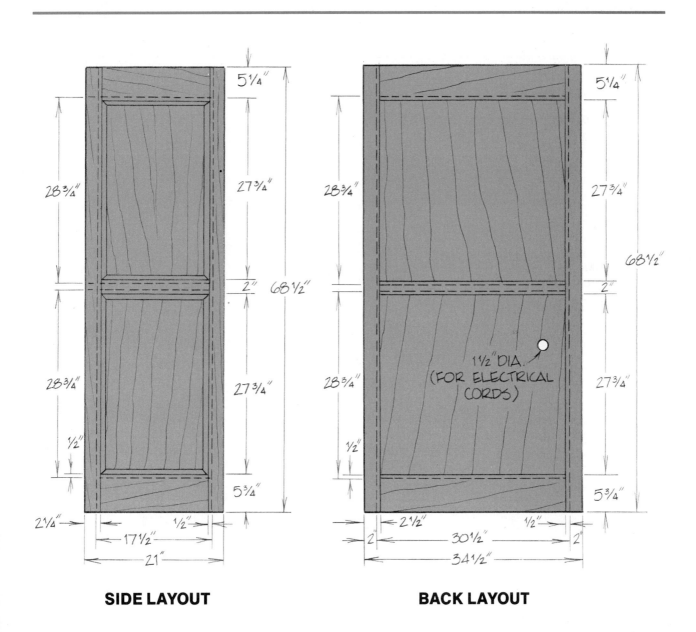

SIDE LAYOUT   **BACK LAYOUT**

6 Assemble the case.

6 **Assemble the case.** With a helper, stand the frames up on a flat surface, forming a box. Hold the box together temporarily with band clamps. Align the frames with the corners square and flush.

Step inside the box and install trapeze fittings to hold the frames together, as shown in *Section A* and *Section B*. (See Figure 4.) The placement of these fittings is not critical, but you should use at least three at each front corner (top, middle, bottom) and two at each back corner (top, middle). Think ahead — place the fittings where they won't interfere with the shelving supports or the drawer unit that you will install later.

Secure the bottom of each back corner with a flathead wood screw, driving the screw through the back stile and into the side stile. Because you won't be able to reach these corners after the drawer unit is installed, you must use screws instead of trapeze fittings.

4/You can purchase trapeze fittings from most mail-order hardware suppliers.

½" WD GROOVE

2¼"

28¹¹⁄₁₆"

27¹¹⁄₁₆"

2"

61⁷⁄₈"

28¹¹⁄₁₆"

27¹¹⁄₁₆"

½"

2¼"

2¼"   ½"

11⅛"

14⅝"

DOOR LAYOUT

CROWN MOLDING

BEAD MOLDING

STOP MOLDING

2" 1"DIA (TYP)

VENTILATION HOLES

¾"

26¼"

GLUE BLOCKS

43"

TOP VIEW

BEAD MOLDING

¾"

GLUE BLOCKS

24"

BACK SUPPORT   ¾"

37½"

BOTTOM VIEW

7

Cut the parts for the bottom and the top sections. Measure the outside of the case, make adjustments necessary to the dimensions of the bottom and top, and cut them out. Rip the molding stock to the proper width, but do *not* cut it to length yet. Wait until you have cut the molding profiles.

8

Make the top and bottom moldings. The *kas* has four different moldings — bead, cove, crown, and stop. You made one of them — the stop molding — when you ripped and planed ½"-thick, 1"-wide strips of stock. The other three require further work.

Bead and cove moldings — Make the top and bottom bead and cove moldings with a shaper, router, or table saw-mounted molding head. Use a ½"-radius quarter-round cutter to form the bead, and a ½"-radius cove cutter to form the cove. Note that the bead molding includes a ¼"-wide step, as shown in the *Top Molding Detail* and *Bottom Molding Detail*. While the bead molding is at hand, cut or rout ¾"-wide, ⅜"-deep grooves on the *inside* face of it. These grooves fit over the top and bottom, holding the molding assemblies in place.

Crown molding — Since it does not incorporate an ogee shape, this isn't a true classical crown molding. It is a traditional *country* crown molding, used frequently by German and Scandinavian craftsmen. It is simply a flat board with chamfered edges. Cut the chamfers on a table saw, with the blade tilted to 45°. Cut the ¼"-wide chamfers first, then the wider ones.

Finally, cut 13 triangular glue blocks from ¾" stock to reinforce the crown molding.

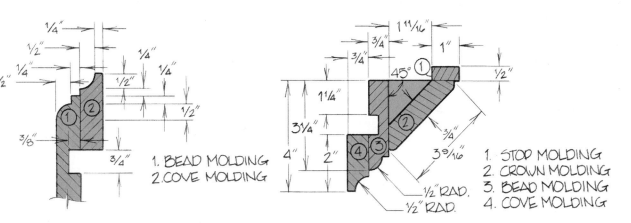

BOTTOM MOLDING DETAIL

1. BEAD MOLDING
2. COVE MOLDING

TOP MOLDING DETAIL

1. STOP MOLDING
2. CROWN MOLDING
3. BEAD MOLDING
4. COVE MOLDING

9

Cut the shape of the bracket feet. The bottom bead molding is cut to form bracket feet when the bottom section is assembled. First, cut the molding to fit the bottom, mitering the ends where the molding strips join. Enlarge the *Side Feet Pattern* and *Front Feet Pattern* and trace them onto the molding stock. Cut out the shapes with a band saw or saber saw, then sand the sawed edges.

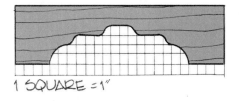

1 SQUARE = 1"

FRONT FEET PATTERN

SIDE FEET PATTERN

10

Assemble the top and bottom sections. Drill ventilation holes in the top. Finish sand all the molding stock, then apply it in layers. Start with the bead molding. Cut the top bead molding to length, mitering the adjoining ends. Glue the bead moldings to the edges of the top and bottom. (The top and bottom fit in the grooves in the bead moldings.) Attach the back support with glue. Reinforce the miter joints and the butt joints on the bottom section with glue blocks.

Cut the cove molding to fit *inside* the bead molding. Once again, miter adjoining ends. Put the cove molding in place, and measure the inside dimensions of the top and the bottom. Remember, the case must fit inside the molding. There should be a 1/32"-1/16" gap between the outside surface of the case and the inside surface of the molding. If the fit will be too tight, plane a little stock from the inside of the cove moldings. If it will be too loose, you may have to remake the molding from thicker stock. When you're satisfied with the fit, glue the cove molding in place.

Cut the crown molding, mitering adjoining ends. Making the compound miter required is tricky. The most accurate way to do it is with a two-board V-jig attached to the table saw's miter gauge. Place the molding in the jig with the wide chamfered edges flat against the base and the upright. Adjust the angle of the miter gauge to 45°, then cut the molding. (See Figure 5.)

Glue the crown molding to the top assembly, and reinforce the glue joints with the triangular glue blocks. After the glue dries, cut the stop molding and glue it to the top chamfered edge of the crown molding.

5/Attach a V-jig to the miter gauge to hold the crown molding while you cut it. The jig should be long enough to extend past the blade. When you cut the molding, you also cut the jig. (Sawguard removed for clarity.)

11

Attach the top and bottom to the case. Put the top on the case, and attach it with four trapeze fittings. With a helper, lay the case down on its back. Put the bottom in place and secure it by driving four flathead wood screws through the bottom and into the bottom rails of the sides. (You can't use trapeze fittings to install the bottom, because you can't get at them when the drawer unit is in place.)

12

Cut the parts for the shelves and drawers. Measure the interior of the completed case, and make any adjustments necessary to the dimensions of the shelves and drawer unit. Take the dimensions of the extension slides into consideration.

As drawn, there is a 1/2" space between the sides of the drawers and drawer supports for the slides. If your slides need more or less space, make the necessary adjustments to the dimensions. Once you're certain of your dimensions, cut the remaining parts to size.

13

Assemble the drawer unit. The drawer unit is a box held together by 3/4"-wide, 3/8"-deep dado joints. Cut the dadoes with a dado cutter, then assemble the drawer unit top, bottom, supports, and braces with glue and screws. Cover the exposed plies with veneer tape or thin wood strips.

If you want, install a TV pullout with swivel in the *kas*. (See Figure 6.) With the doors open, the TV can be pulled clear of the case and swiveled from side to side to provide unobstructed viewing. Bolt it to the top of the drawer unit at this time.

6/Purchase a swivel/ pullout with at least a 100-pound capacity. These are available from many mail-order hardware suppliers.

14

Build and install the drawers. Cut the joinery in the drawer parts. Join the fronts and backs to the sides with ⅜″-long half-blind dovetails. Float the drawer bottom in ¼″-wide, ⅜″-deep grooves. You can cut the dovetails with a router and a dovetail jig. Cut the grooves with a router or a dado cutter.

Finish sand the drawer parts, and dry assemble them to check the fit. Measure the drawers to make sure they will fit in the drawer unit. If everything fits, reassemble the drawers, including the faces, with glue. Do *not* glue the drawer bottoms; let them float in the grooves. Be sure the drawers remain square as you apply the clamps.

When the glue dries, cut handholds in the top edge of the drawer faces/fronts with a saber saw. Sand the sawed edges.

Install the extension slides. Most slides separate so you can attach one part to the drawer, and the other to the case. Fit the drawer in the case following the slide manufacturer's instructions. Check the sliding action; if a drawer binds, you may have to adjust the slides.

15

Install the drawer unit in the case. Undo the top and back trapeze fittings, and remove the screws from the bottom back corners. Remove the top and the back from the case, and place the drawer unit inside. Rest the front of the unit on the front bottom rest. Tilt it forward slightly while you replace the back, then let it settle on the back bottom rest. Replace the top section, then secure the trapeze fittings and screws.

Note: There is no need to secure the drawer unit inside the case. Because of its weight, it will remain in place without screws or other fasteners.

16

Build and install the adjustable shelves. Lay out and drill a sequence of ¼″-diameter holes through the shelving supports. To ensure the supports are exactly the same, stack them up and drill all four parts simultaneously. The holes should be spaced every 2″, as shown in *Section B*.

Cover the fronts of the shelves with veneer tape or thin wood strips to hide the plies. Attach the shelving supports to the side sections with flathead wood screws, as shown in *Section B*. Insert metal pin-supports in the holes, and lay the shelves on the pins.

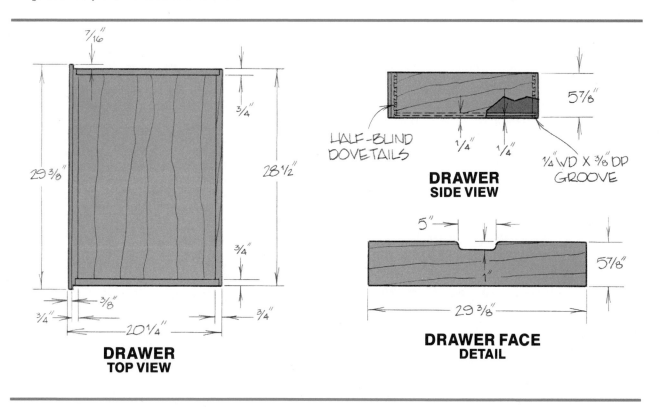

DRAWER
TOP VIEW

DRAWER
SIDE VIEW

DRAWER FACE
DETAIL

17 Mount the doors.

Wedge the doors in place to test their fit. Plane or scrape the edges if they seem too tight. Then hinge them to the front frame.

We used rat-tail hinges, which are typical of country furniture. Rat-tail hinges, forged by blacksmiths, were made until the industrial advances of the nineteenth century made inexpensive butt hinges commonplace. The advantage of rat-tails on a project like this is that they make it easy to remove the doors. You lift the leaves off the rat-tail posts. (See Figure 7.) This makes it possible for you to store the doors out of the way when you want to watch television. You can still purchase hand-forged rat-tail hinges from:

Ball and Ball
463 W. Lincoln Highway
Exton, PA 19341

Install door pulls near the middle of the inside door stiles, and put catches on *both* the top and the bottom door stops to keep the doors flush in the case. Without both catches, they might warp and look sprung.

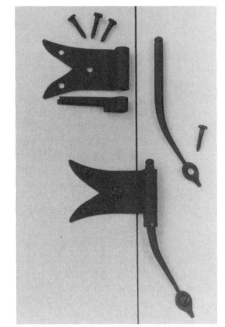

7/A rat-tail hinge consists of a leaf, a post, and a collar. Mount the leaf on the door, and the post and collar on the case. To remove the door from the case, simply lift the leaf off the post.

18 Finish the completed "kas."

Disassemble all the sections of the *kas,* and remove the doors from the front frame. Remove all the hinges, trapeze fittings, door pulls, and other hardware. Do any touch-up sanding necessary, then apply a finish. Be sure to coat the inside and outside surfaces equally — this will help keep the parts from warping or distorting. When the finish dries, carry the sections to wherever you intend to put the *kas* and reassemble it on the spot.

Electronics and Wood

Storing audio and video equipment in a wooden cabinet creates problems for both the equipment and the cabinet. The equipment generates heat when it's turned on. If the cabinet isn't properly ventilated, the heat may build up and damage the electronic components. It will also dry the wood, causing it to split and crack.

There are several simple steps you can take to prevent this:

■ Ventilate the cabinet at the *top.* Hot air rises. Even with the doors open, a cabinet with a solid top may overheat. Drill holes or make openings in the top to let the heat escape.

■ Allow air flow *around* the shelves. Shelves that are mounted solidly to the sides and back of a cabinet will trap heat beneath them. Drill holes in the shelves, or leave space at the back or sides to let the heat rise.

■ If you light the interior of the cabinet, use *fluorescent* lights. Lumen for lumen, fluorescent bulbs generate only 5% of the heat created by a comparable incandescent.

■ Use *frame and panel* construction, so that the wood can expand and contract freely. This construction also helps to counteract the internal tension that's present in every board, keeping the cabinet from warping or distorting. Avoid large expanses of solid wood that must be securely fastened in place.

■ Apply as many coats of finish to the *inside* of the cabinet as to the outside. If you don't, one side will absorb and release moisture faster than the other. The wood will swell and shrink unevenly, distorting the cabinet. Eventually, the wood will split.

■ Wax the cabinet more frequently than usual. Heat dries natural oils in the wood, leaving it brittle. Wax will replenish some of the oils.

Credits

Contributing Craftsmen and Craftswomen:

    David Calhoun (Rocking Chair)

    Nick Engler (Joiner's Wing-and-Arm Chair, Pipebox, Fretwork Mirror, Tilt-Top Candlestand, Lap Desk, Audio/Video *Kas*)

    Mary Jane Favorite (Joiner's Wing-and-Arm Chair, Pipebox, Fretwork Mirror, Tilt-Top Candlestand, Pewter Bench, Uncle Sam Whirligig, Game Board, Weathervanes)

    Robert Pinter (Windsor Settee)

    Stephen Wright (Writing Dcsk)

    Chris Walendzak (Uncle Sam Whirligig)

    Note: Several of the projects in this book were built by country craftsmen whose names have been erased by time. We regret that we cannot tell you who built them; we can only admire their craftsmanship. These pieces include the Occasional Table, Mantle Clock, and Sailmaker's Bench.

The designs for the newer projects in this book (those attributed to a designer or builder) are the copyrighted property of the craftsmen and craftswomen who built them. Readers are encouraged to reproduce these projects for their personal use or for gifts. However, reproduction for sale or profit is forbidden by law.

Special Thanks To:

    Mr. and Mrs. Nicholas Engler, Jr.

    Wertz Hardware Stores, West Milton, Ohio

    The Workshops of David T. Smith, Morrow, Ohio

Rodale Press, Inc., publishes AMERICAN WOODWORKER™, the magazine for the serious woodworking hobbyist. For information on how to order your subscription, write to AMERICAN WOODWORKER™, Emmaus, PA 18098.